I0814152

PEACE BE WITH YOU!

PEACE BE WITH YOU!

MY WORDS TO THE CHURCH AND TO THE WORLD

POPE LEO XIV

HARPERONE
An Imprint of HarperCollins*Publishers*

Chapter titles have been added by the editor.

 For information, address HarperCollins Publishers, 195 Broadway, New York, NY 10007. In Europe, HarperCollins Publishers, Macken House, 39/40 Mayor Street Upper, Dublin 1, D01 C9W8, Ireland.

HarperCollins books may be purchased for educational, business, or sales promotional use. For information, please email the Special Markets Department at SPsales@harpercollins.com.

hc.com

Originally published as *E pace sia!: Parole alla Chiesa e al mondo* in 2025 by Dicastero per la Comunicazione—Libreria Editrice Vaticana.

First HarperOne hardcover published in 2026.

Designed by Yvonne Chan

Library of Congress Cataloging-in-Publication Data has been applied for.

ISBN 978-0-06-351481-2

Printed in the United States of America

25 26 27 28 29 LBC 5 4 3 2 1

Contents

CONTENTS

CONTENTS

Foreword

Peace is one of the great issues of our time and is both a gift and a commitment: a gift from God built by men and women throughout the ages.

We live in a world wounded by too many conflicts and struck by bloody hostilities. Bitter nationalism tramples on the rights of the weakest. Even before it is crushed on the battlefield, peace is defeated in the human heart when we give in to selfishness and greed and when we allow partisan interests to prevail instead of looking to the common good. Many writers have said that it is when we refuse to listen to other people's stories that we begin to deprive them of their dignity. Depersonalizing others is the first step in any war. To know others, on the other hand, is a foretaste of peace. But in order to know, one must first know how to love. Saint Augustine said that "no one can be known except through friendship" (*Eighty-three Different Questions*, 71).

I would like to reflect here on this dual dimension of peace, which is vertical (peace as a gift from Above) and horizontal (peace as the responsibility of each person).

Peace is a gift that God has given to men and women of every age through Jesus' birth in Bethlehem. The angels announced peace on earth because God became man. He embraced humanity so deeply that with his cross, he destroyed the enmity of sin. Saint Augustine writes: "We, too, shall be a source of additional glory to God in the highest when, after the resurrection of our spiritual body, we shall be lifted up in the clouds to meet Christ, on condition, of course, that we work for peace with good will while we are here on earth" (*Sermons*, 193). The glory of God descended upon the earth to make us participants in his infinite goodness. This gift calls into action the responsibility of our answer, of our "good will", as the Saint of Hippo writes.

Furthermore, peace is the gift that the Risen One gave to his disciples. It is a peace "injured" by the wounds of the crucifixion, because Jesus' peace gushes forth from a heart that loves and lets itself be struck by the suffering of every time and place. "The Lord appeared to His disciples after His resurrection, as ye have heard, and saluted them, saying, 'Peace be unto you.' This is peace indeed, and the salutation of salvation: for the very word salutation has received its name from salvation" (Saint Augustine, *Sermons*, 116).

However, peace is also a commitment and responsibility for each one of us. Peace means teaching children to respect others and not to bully others when they play. Peace means overcoming our personal pride and making room for the other, in our family, at work, in sports. Peace is when our heart and our life are inhabited by silence, meditation, and listening to God; because God never blesses violence, he never approves of taking advantage of others, or of the frenzied abuse of the one Earth that is disfiguring Creation, a caress of the Creator.

We may feel powerless before the many wars being fought around the world. We can respond in various ways to what I called the 'globalization of powerlessness': believers can, first and foremost, give voice to prayer. Prayer is an "unarmed" force that seeks only the common good, without exclusions. By praying, we disarm our ego and become capable of gratuitousness and sincerity.

Moreover, our heart is the most important battlefield. It is there that we must learn the bloodless but necessary victory over the impulses of death and the tendencies toward domination: only peaceful hearts can build a world of peace. We must practice a culture of reconciliation by creating non-violent workshops, places where suspicion of others can become an opportunity for encounter. The heart is the source of peace: there we must learn to meet rather than clash with each other, to trust and not mistrust, to listen and understand instead of closing ourselves to others.

Finally, politics and the international community are responsible for facilitating the mediation of conflicts, utilizing the arts of dialogue and diplomacy. "O Lord God, grant your peace to us . . . , the peace of rest, the peace of the Sabbath which has no evening": with these words of Augustine, let us ask the Father to grant our world, all people, especially those who are most forgotten and who suffer the most, the blessing grace of a just and lasting peace.

Leo PP. XIV

Vatican City, December 6th, 2025

PEACE
BE WITH
YOU!

Unarmed and Disarming Peace

First Apostolic Blessing Urbi et Orbi

CENTRAL LOGGIA OF THE VATICAN BASILICA

THURSDAY, MAY 8, 2025

Peace be with you all!

Dear brothers and sisters, these are the first words spoken by the Risen Christ, the Good Shepherd who laid down his life for God's flock. I would like this greeting of peace to resound in your hearts, in your families, among all people, wherever they may be, in every nation and throughout the world. Peace be with you!

It is the peace of the Risen Christ. A peace that is unarmed and disarming, humble and persevering. A peace that comes from God, the God who loves us all, unconditionally.

We can still hear the faint yet ever courageous voice of Pope Francis as he blessed Rome, the Pope who blessed Rome, who gave his blessing to the world, the whole world, on the morning of Easter.

Allow me to extend that same blessing: God loves us, God loves you all, and evil will not prevail! All of us are in God's hands. So, let us move forward, without fear, together, hand in hand with God and with one another other! We are followers of Christ. Christ goes before us. The world needs his light. Humanity needs him as the bridge that can lead us to God and his love. Help us, one and all, to build bridges through dialogue and encounter, joining together as one people, always at peace. Thank you, Pope Francis!

I also thank my brother cardinals, who have chosen me to be the Successor of Peter and to walk together with you as a Church, united, ever pursuing peace and justice, ever seeking to act as men and women faithful to Jesus Christ, in order to proclaim the Gospel without fear, to be missionaries.

I am an Augustinian, a son of Saint Augustine, who once said, "With you I am a Christian, and for you I am a bishop."* In this sense, all of us can journey together toward the homeland that God has prepared for us.

A special greeting to the Church of Rome! Together, we must look for ways to be a missionary

---

* Saint Augustine of Hippo, *Sermons*, 340, 1.

Church, a Church that builds bridges and encourages dialogue, a Church ever open to welcoming, like this square with its open arms, all those who are in need of our charity, our presence, our readiness to dialogue and our love.

And if you also allow me a brief word, a greeting to everyone and in particular to my beloved Diocese of Chiclayo, in Peru, where a faithful people has accompanied its bishop, shared its faith, and given so much, so much, to continue being a faithful Church of Jesus Christ.

To all of you, brothers and sisters in Rome, in Italy, throughout the world: We want to be a synodal Church, a Church that moves forward, a Church that always seeks peace, that always seeks charity, that always seeks to be close above all to those who are suffering.

Today is the day of the Prayer of Supplication to Our Lady of Pompeii. Our Mother Mary always wants to walk at our side, to remain close to us, to help us with her intercession and her love. So I would like to pray together with you. Let us pray together for this new mission, for the whole Church, for peace in the world, and let us ask Mary, our Mother, for this special grace: *Hail Mary . . .*

Joyful Witnesses

Homily for the Holy Mass Pro Ecclesia
Celebrated with the Cardinals

SISTINE CHAPEL

FRIDAY, MAY 9, 2025

I want to repeat the words from the responsorial Psalm: "I will sing a new song to the Lord, because he has done marvels" (Ps 98:1).

And indeed, not just with me but with all of us. My brother cardinals, as we celebrate this morning, I invite you to recognize the marvels that the Lord has done, the blessings that the Lord continues to pour out on all of us through the ministry of Peter.

You have called me to carry that cross and to be blessed with that mission, and I know I can rely on each and every one of you to walk with me, as we continue as a Church, as a community of friends of Jesus, as believers to announce the Good News, to announce the Gospel.

"You are the Christ, the Son of the living God" (Mt 16:16). With these words, Peter, when asked by the Master, together with the other disciples, about his faith in him, expressed the patrimony that the Church, through the apostolic succession, has preserved, deepened, and handed on for two thousand years.

Jesus is the Christ, the Son of the living God: the one Savior, who alone reveals the face of the Father.

In him, God, in order to make himself close and accessible to men and women, revealed himself to us in the trusting eyes of a child, in the lively mind of a young person, and in the mature features of a man,* finally appearing to his disciples after the resurrection with his glorious body. He thus showed us a model of human holiness that we can all imitate, together with the promise of an eternal destiny that transcends all our limits and abilities.

Peter, in his response, understands both of these things: the gift of God and the path to follow in order to allow himself to be changed by that gift. They are two inseparable aspects of salvation entrusted to the Church to be proclaimed for the good of the

* Cf. Vatican II, Pastoral Constitution *Gaudium et Spes* on the Church in the Modern World, December 7, 1965, 22.

human race. Indeed, they are entrusted to us, who were chosen by him before we were formed in our mothers' wombs (cf. Jer 1:5), reborn in the waters of baptism, and, surpassing our limitations and with no merit of our own, brought here and sent forth from here, so that the Gospel might be proclaimed to every creature (cf. Mk 16:15).

In a particular way, God has called me by your election to succeed the Prince of the Apostles and has entrusted this treasure to me so that, with his help, I may be its faithful administrator (cf. 1 Cor 4:2) for the sake of the entire mystical Body of the Church. He has done so in order that she may be ever more fully a city set on a hill (cf. Mt 5:14), an ark of salvation sailing through the waters of history, and a beacon that illumines the dark nights of this world. And this, not so much through the magnificence of her structures or the grandeur of her buildings—like the monuments among which we find ourselves—but rather through the holiness of her members. For we are the people whom God has chosen as his own, so that we may declare the wonderful deeds of him who called us out of darkness into his marvelous light (cf. 1 Pt 2:9).

Peter, however, makes his profession of faith in reply to a specific question: "Who do people say that the Son of Man is?" (Mt 16:13). The question is not insignificant. It concerns an essential aspect of our ministry, namely, the world in which we live, with its limitations and its potential, its questions and its convictions.

"Who do people say that the Son of Man is?" If we reflect on the scene we are considering, we might find two possible answers, which characterize two different attitudes.

First, there is the world's response. Matthew tells us that this conversation between Jesus and his disciples takes place in the beautiful town of Caesarea Philippi, filled with luxurious palaces, set in a magnificent natural landscape at the foot of Mount Hermon, but also a place of cruel power plays and the scene of betrayals and infidelity. This setting speaks to us of a world that considers Jesus a completely insignificant person, at best someone with an unusual and striking way of speaking and acting. And so, once his presence becomes irksome because of his demands for honesty and his stern moral requirements, this "world" will not hesitate to reject and eliminate him.

Then there is the other possible response to Jesus's question: that of ordinary people. For them, the Nazarene is not a charlatan, but an upright man, one who has courage, who speaks well and says the right things, like other great prophets in the history of Israel. That is why they follow him, at least for as long as they can do so without too much risk or inconvenience. Yet to them he is only a man, and therefore, in times of danger, during his passion, they too abandon him and depart disappointed.

What is striking about these two attitudes is their relevance today. They embody notions that we could easily find on the lips of many men and women in our own time, even if, while essentially identical, they are expressed in different language.

Even today, there are many settings in which the Christian faith is considered absurd, meant for the weak and unintelligent. Settings where other securities are preferred, like technology, money, success, power, or pleasure.

These are contexts where it is not easy to preach the Gospel and bear witness to its truth, where believers are mocked, opposed, despised, or at best tolerated and pitied. Yet, precisely for this reason, they are the places where our missionary outreach is desperately needed.

A lack of faith is often tragically accompanied by the loss of meaning in life, the neglect of mercy, appalling violations of human dignity, the crisis of the family, and so many other wounds that afflict our society.

Today, too, there are many settings in which Jesus, although appreciated as a man, is reduced to a kind of charismatic leader or superman. This is true not only among nonbelievers but also among many baptized Christians, who thus end up living, at this level, in a state of practical atheism.

This is the world that has been entrusted to us, a world in which, as Pope Francis taught us so many times, we are called to bear witness to our joyful faith in Jesus the Savior. Therefore, it is essential that we too repeat, with Peter, "You are the Christ, the Son of the living God" (Mt 16:16).

It is essential to do this, first of all, in our personal relationship with the Lord, in our commitment to a daily journey of conversion. Then, to do so as a Church, experiencing together our fidelity to the Lord and bringing the Good News to all.*

---

* Cf. Vatican II, Dogmatic Constitution on the Church *Lumen Gentium*, November 21, 1964, 1.

I say this first of all to myself, as the Successor of Peter, as I begin my mission as Bishop of Rome and, according to the well-known expression of Saint Ignatius of Antioch, am called to preside in charity over the universal Church.* Saint Ignatius, who was led in chains to this city, the place of his impending sacrifice, wrote to the Christians there: "Then I will truly be a disciple of Jesus Christ, when the world no longer sees my body."† Ignatius was speaking about being devoured by wild beasts in the arena—and so it happened—but his words apply more generally to an indispensable commitment for all those in the Church who exercise a ministry of authority. It is to move aside so that Christ may remain, to make oneself small so that he may be known and glorified (cf. Jn 3:30), to spend oneself to the utmost so that all may have the opportunity to know and love him.

May God grant me this grace, today and always, through the loving intercession of Mary, Mother of the Church.

* Cf. Saint Ignatius of Antioch, *Letter to the Romans*, Prologue.
† Ibid., IV, 1.

Prayer and Commitment

Address to the College of Cardinals

SYNODAL HALL

SATURDAY, MAY 10, 2025

I greet all of you with gratitude for this meeting and for the days that preceded it. Days that were sad because of the loss of the Holy Father Pope Francis and demanding due to the responsibilities we confronted together, yet at the same time, in accordance with the promise Jesus himself made to us, days rich in grace and consolation in the Spirit (cf. Jn 14:25–27).

You, dear cardinals, are the closest collaborators of the Pope. This has proved a great comfort to me in accepting a yoke clearly far beyond my own limited powers, as it would be for any of us. Your presence reminds me that the Lord, who has entrusted me with this mission, will not leave me alone in bearing its responsibility. I know, before all else, that I can always count on his help, the help of the Lord, and through his grace and providence, on your closeness and that of so many of our brothers and sisters throughout the world who believe in God, love the Church, and support the Vicar of Christ by their prayers and good works.

I thank the Dean of the College of Cardinals, Cardinal Giovanni Battista Re—who deserves applause, at least once, if not more—whose wisdom, the fruit of a long life and many years of faithful service to the Apostolic See, has helped us greatly during this time. I thank the Camerlengo of the Holy Roman Church, Cardinal Kevin Joseph Farrell—I believe he is present today—for the important and demanding work that he has done throughout the period of the vacant see and for the convocation of the conclave. My thoughts also go to our brother cardinals who, for reasons of health, were unable to be present, and I join you in embracing them in communion of affection and prayer.

At this moment, both sad and joyful, providentially bathed in the light of Easter, I would like all of us to see the passing of our beloved Holy Father Pope Francis and the conclave as a paschal event, a stage in that long exodus through which the Lord continues to guide us toward the fullness of life. In this perspective, we entrust to the "merciful Father and God of all consolation" (2 Cor 1:3) the soul of the late Pontiff and also the future of the Church.

Beginning with Saint Peter and up to myself, his unworthy successor, the Pope has been a humble servant of God and of his brothers and sisters, and nothing more than this. It has been clearly seen in the example of so many of my predecessors, and most recently by Pope Francis himself, with his example of complete dedication to service and to sober simplicity of life, his abandonment to God throughout his ministry, and his serene trust at the moment of his return to the Father's house. Let us take up this precious legacy and continue on the journey, inspired by the same hope that is born of faith.

It is the Risen Lord, present among us, who protects and guides the Church and continues to fill her with hope through the love "poured into our hearts through the Holy Spirit who has been given to us" (Rom 5:5). It is up to us to be docile listeners to his voice and faithful ministers of his plan of salvation, mindful that God loves to communicate himself, not in the roar of thunder and earthquakes, but in the "whisper of a gentle breeze" (1 Kgs 19:12) or, as some translate it, in a "sound of sheer silence." It is this essential and important encounter to which we must guide and accompany all the holy people of God entrusted to our care.

In these days, we have been able to see the beauty and feel the strength of this immense community, which with such affection and devotion has greeted and mourned its shepherd, accompanying him with faith and prayer at the time of his final encounter with the Lord. We have seen the true grandeur of the Church, which is alive in the rich variety of her members in union with her one Head, Christ, "the shepherd and guardian" (1 Pt 2:25) of our souls. She is the womb from which we were born and at the same time the flock (cf. Jn 21:15–17), the field (cf. Mk 4:1–20) entrusted to us to protect and cultivate, to nourish with the sacraments of salvation and to make fruitful by our sowing the seed of the Word, so that, steadfast in one accord and enthusiastic in mission, she may press forward, like the Israelites in the desert, in the shadow of the cloud and in the light of God's fire (cf. Ex 13:21).

In this regard, I would like us to renew together today our complete commitment to the path that the universal Church has now followed for decades in the wake of the Second Vatican Council. Pope Francis masterfully and concretely set it forth in the apostolic exhortation *Evangelii Gaudium*, from which I would like to highlight several fundamental points: the return to the primacy of Christ in proclamation; the missionary conversion of the entire Christian community; growth in collegiality and synodality; attention to the *sensus fidei* (the sense of the faith), especially in its most authentic and inclusive forms, such as popular piety; loving care for the least and the rejected;* and courageous and trusting dialogue with the contemporary world in its various components and realities.†

These are evangelical principles that have always inspired and guided the life and activity of God's family. In these values, the merciful face of the Father

---

* Cf. Francis, Apostolic Exhortation *Evangelii Gaudium*, on the Proclamation of the Gospel in Today's World, November 24, 2013, 11, 9, 33, 119–120, 123, 53.

† Cf. Vatican II, Pastoral Constitution *Gaudium et Spes*, on the Church in the Modern World, December 7, 1965, 1–2.

has been revealed and continues to be revealed in his incarnate Son, the ultimate hope of all who sincerely seek truth, justice, peace, and fraternity.*

Sensing myself called to continue in this same path, I chose to take the name Leo XIV. There are different reasons for this, but mainly because Pope Leo XIII in his historic encyclical *Rerum Novarum* addressed the social question in the context of the first great Industrial Revolution. In our own day, the Church offers to everyone the treasury of her social teaching in response to another industrial revolution and to developments in the field of artificial intelligence that pose new challenges for the defense of human dignity, justice, and labor.

Dear brothers, I would like to conclude the first part of our meeting by making my own—and proposing to you as well—the hope that Saint Paul VI expressed at the inauguration of his Petrine ministry in 1963: "May it pass over the whole world like a great flame of faith and love kindled in all men and women of good will. May it shed light on paths of

---

* Cf. Benedict XVI, Encyclical Letter *Spe Salvi* on Christian Hope, November 30, 2007, 2; Francis, Bull of Indiction of the Ordinary Jubilee of the Year 2025, *Spes non Confundit*, May 9, 2024, 3.

mutual cooperation and bless humanity abundantly, now and always, with the very strength of God, without whose help nothing is valid, nothing is holy."*

May these also be our sentiments, to be translated into prayer and commitment, with the Lord's help. Thank you!

* Saint Paul VI, Message *Qui Fausto Die* Addressed to the Entire Human Family, June 22, 1963.

From Listening to Service

Homily for the Mass in the Crypt of Saint Peter's Basilica

VATICAN GROTTOES

SUNDAY, MAY 11, 2025

The Gospel that we just heard on this Sunday of the Good Shepherd: "My sheep listen to my voice; I know them, and they follow me" (Jn 10:27).

I think about the Good Shepherd, especially on this Sunday, which is so significant in Easter time. While we celebrate the beginning of this new mission of the ministry that the Church has called me to, there is no better example than Jesus Christ himself, to whom we give our lives and on whom we depend. Jesus Christ whom we follow, he is the Good Shepherd, and he is the one who gives us life: the way and the truth and the life. So we celebrate with joy this day, and we deeply appreciate your presence here.

Today is Mother's Day. I think there is only one

mother present: Happy Mother's Day! One of the most wonderful expressions of the love of God is the love that is poured out by mothers, especially to their children and grandchildren.

This Sunday is known to be special for several different reasons: One of the first ones I would mention is vocations. During the recent work of the cardinals, before and after the election of the new Pope, we spoke a lot about vocations in the Church and how important it is that all of us search together. First and foremost by giving a good example in our lives, with joy, living the joy of the Gospel, not discouraging others, but rather looking for ways to encourage young people to hear the voice of the Lord and to follow it and to serve in the Church. "I am the Good Shepherd," he tells us.

Now I will add just a word also in Italian, because this mission we carry forward is no longer to a single diocese, but to all the Church: This universal spirit is important. And we also find it in the first reading we heard (Acts 13, 14:43–52). Paul and Barnabas go to Antioch; the Jews go first, but they do not want to listen to the voice of the Lord, and so they begin to announce the Gospel to all the world, to the pagans. They go, as we know, on this great mission. Saint Paul comes to Rome, where he also eventually fulfilled it. Another example of the witness of a good shepherd. But in that example, there is also a very special invitation to us all. I also said it in a very personal way, what it is to proclaim the Gospel to the whole world.

Take courage! Without fear! Many times in the Gospel Jesus says, "Do not be afraid." We need to be courageous in the witness we give, with the world and above all with life: giving life, serving, sometimes with great sacrifices in order to live out this very mission.

I saw a little reflection that made me think a lot, because it also comes out in the Gospel. In this sense, someone asked, "When you think about your life, how do you explain where you have arrived?" The answer they gave in this reflection is in a certain sense mine too, with the verb "to listen." How important it is to listen! Jesus says, "My sheep listen to my voice" (Jn 10:27). And I think it is important for all of us to learn how to listen more, to enter into dialogue. First and foremost, with the Lord: Always listen to the Word of God. Then also listen to others, to know how to build bridges, to know how to listen without judging, not closing the doors thinking that we have all the truth and no one else can tell us anything. It is very important to listen to the voice of the Lord, to listen to it, in this dialogue, and to see where the Lord is calling us toward.

Walking together in the Church, let us ask the Lord to give us this grace of being able to listen to his Word, to serve all his people.

“No” to the War of Words

Address to Representatives of the Media

AUDIENCE HALL

MONDAY, MAY 12, 2025

I welcome you, representatives of the media from around the world. Thank you for the work you have done and continue to do in these days, which is truly a time of grace for the Church.

In the Sermon on the Mount, Jesus proclaimed, "Blessed are the peacemakers" (Mt 5:9). This is a beatitude that challenges all of us, but it is particularly relevant to you, calling each one of you to strive for a different kind of communication, one that does not seek consensus at all costs, does not use aggressive words, does not follow the culture of competition, and never separates the search for truth from the love with which we must humbly seek it. Peace begins with each one of us: in the way we look at others, listen to others, and speak about others. In this sense, the way we communicate is of fundamental importance: We must say "no" to the war of words and images; we must reject the paradigm of war.

Let me therefore reiterate today the Church's solidarity with journalists who are imprisoned for seeking to report the truth, and with these words I also ask for the release of these imprisoned journalists. The Church recognizes in these witnesses—I am thinking of those who report on war even at the cost of their lives—the courage of those who defend dignity, justice, and the right of people to be informed, because only informed individuals can make free choices. The suffering of these imprisoned journalists challenges the conscience of nations and the international community, calling on all of us to safeguard the precious gift of free speech and of the press.

Thank you, dear friends, for your service to the truth. You have been in Rome these past few weeks to report on the Church, its diversity, and, at the same time, its unity. You were present during the liturgies of Holy Week and then reported on the sorrow felt over the death of Pope Francis, which nevertheless took place in the light of Easter. That same Easter faith drew us into the spirit of the conclave, during which you worked long and tiring days. Yet, even on this occasion, you managed to recount the beauty of Christ's love that unites and makes us one people, guided by the Good Shepherd.

We are living in times that are difficult both to navigate and to recount. They present a challenge for all of us, but it is one that we should not run away from. On the contrary, they demand that each one of us, in our different roles and services, never give in to mediocrity. The Church must face the challenges posed by the times. In the same way, communication and journalism do not exist outside of time and history. Saint Augustine reminds of this when he said, "Let us live well and the times will be good. We are the times."*

Thank you, therefore, for what you have done to move beyond stereotypes and clichés through which we often interpret Christian life and the life of the Church itself. Thank you because you have captured the essence of who we are and conveyed it to the whole world through every form of media possible.

Today, one of the most important challenges is to promote communication that can bring us out of the

* Saint Augustine of Hippo, *Sermons*, 80, 8.

"Tower of Babel" in which we sometimes find ourselves, out of the confusion of loveless languages that are often ideological or partisan. Therefore, your service, with the words you use and the style you adopt, is crucial. As you know, communication is not only the transmission of information, but it is also the creation of a culture, of human and digital environments that become spaces for dialogue and discussion. In looking at how technology is developing, this mission becomes ever more necessary. I am thinking in particular of artificial intelligence, with its immense potential, which nevertheless requires responsibility and discernment in order to ensure that it can be used for the good of all, so that it can benefit all of humanity. This responsibility concerns everyone in proportion to his or her age and role in society.

Dear friends, we will get to know each other better over time. We have experienced—we can say together—truly special days. We have shared them through every form of media: TV, radio, the internet, and social media. I sincerely hope that each of us can say that these days unveiled a little bit of the mystery of our humanity and left us with a desire for love and peace. For this reason, I repeat to you today the invitation made by Pope Francis in his message for this year's World Day of Social Communications: Let us disarm communication of all prejudice and resentment, fanaticism, and even hatred; let us free it from aggression. We do not need loud, forceful communication, but rather communication that is capable of listening and of gathering the voices of the weak who have no voice. Let us disarm words and we will help to disarm the world. Disarmed and disarming communication allows us to share a different view of the world and to act in a manner consistent with our human dignity.

You are at the forefront of reporting on conflicts and aspirations for peace, on situations of injustice and poverty, and on the silent work of so many people striving to create a better world. For this reason, I ask you to choose consciously and courageously the path of communication in favor of peace. Thank you all and may God bless you!

Peace, Justice, Truth

Audience with Members of the Diplomatic Corps Accredited to the Holy See

CLEMENTINE HALL

FRIDAY, MAY 16, 2025

In our dialogue, I would like us always to preserve the sense of being a family. Indeed, the diplomatic community represents the entire family of peoples, a family that shares the joys and sorrows of life and the human and spiritual values that give it meaning and direction. Papal diplomacy is an expression of the very catholicity of the Church. In its diplomatic activity, the Holy See is inspired by a pastoral outreach that leads it not to seek privileges but to strengthen its evangelical mission at the service of humanity. Resisting all forms of indifference, it appeals to consciences, as witnessed by the constant efforts of my venerable predecessor, ever attentive to the cry of the poor, the needy, and the marginalized, as well as to contemporary challenges, ranging from the protection of creation to artificial intelligence.

In addition to being a visible sign of your countries' respect for the Apostolic See, your presence here today is a gift for me. It allows me to renew the Church's aspiration—and my own—to reach out and embrace all individuals and peoples on the Earth, who need and yearn for truth, justice, and peace! In a certain sense, my own life experience, which has spanned North America, South America, and Europe, has been marked by this aspiration to transcend borders in order to encounter different peoples and cultures.

Through the constant and patient work of the Secretariat of State, I intend to strengthen understanding and dialogue with you and with your countries, many of which I have already had the grace to visit, especially during my time as Prior General of the Augustinians. I trust that God's providence will allow me further occasions to get to know the countries from which you come and enable me to have occasions to confirm in the faith our many brothers and sisters throughout the world and to build new bridges with all people of goodwill.

In our dialogue, I would like us to keep in mind

three essential words that represent the pillars of the Church's missionary activity and the aim of the Holy See's diplomacy.

The first word is *peace*. All too often we consider it a "negative" word, indicative only of the absence of war and conflict, since opposition is a perennial part of human nature, frequently leading us to live in a constant "state of conflict" at home, at work, and in society. Peace then appears simply as a respite, a pause between one dispute and another, given that, no matter how hard we try, tensions will always be present, a little like embers burning beneath the ashes, ready to ignite at any moment.

From a Christian perspective—but also in other religious traditions—peace is first and foremost a gift. It is the first gift of Christ: "My peace I give to you" (Jn 14:27). Yet it is an active and demanding gift. It engages and challenges each of us, regardless of our cultural background or religious affiliation, demanding first of all that we work on ourselves. Peace is built in the heart and from the heart, by eliminating pride and vindictiveness and carefully choosing our words. For words too, not only weapons, can wound and even kill.

In this regard, I believe that religions and interreligious dialogue can make a fundamental contribution to fostering a climate of peace. This naturally requires full respect for religious freedom in every country, since religious experience is an essential dimension of the human person. Without it, it is difficult, if not impossible, to bring about the purification of the heart necessary for building peaceful relationships.

This effort, in which all of us are called to take part, can begin to eliminate the root causes of all conflicts and every destructive urge for conquest. It demands a genuine willingness to engage in dialogue, inspired by the desire to communicate rather than clash. As a result, there is a need to give new life to multilateral diplomacy and to those international institutions conceived and designed primarily to remedy eventual disputes within the international community. Naturally, there must also be a resolve to halt the production of instruments of destruction and death, since, as Pope Francis noted in his last *Urbi et Orbi* message: No peace is "possible without true disarmament! The requirement that every people provide for its own defense must not turn into a race to rearmament."*

The second word is *justice*. Working for peace requires acting justly. As I have already mentioned, I chose my name thinking first of all of Leo XIII, the Pope of the first great social encyclical, *Rerum Novarum*. In this time of epochal change, the Holy See cannot fail to make its voice heard in the face of the many imbalances and injustices that lead, not least, to unworthy working conditions and increasingly fragmented and conflict-ridden societies. Every effort should be made to overcome the global inequalities—between opulence and destitution—that are carving deep divides between continents and countries, and even within individual societies.

It is the responsibility of government leaders to work to build harmonious and peaceful civil societies. This can be achieved above all by investing in the family, founded upon the stable union between a man and a woman, "a small but genuine society, and prior

* Francis, Message *Urbi et Orbi*, April 20, 2025.

to all civil society."* In addition, no one is exempted from striving to ensure respect for the dignity of every person, especially the most frail and vulnerable, from the unborn to the elderly, from the sick to the unemployed, citizens and immigrants alike.

My own story is that of a citizen, the descendant of immigrants, who in turn chose to emigrate. All of us, in the course of our lives, can find ourselves healthy or sick, employed or unemployed, living in our native land or in a foreign country, yet our dignity always remains unchanged: It is the dignity of a creature willed and loved by God.

The third word is *truth*. Truly peaceful relationships cannot be built, also within the international community, apart from truth. Where words take on ambiguous and ambivalent connotations, and the virtual world, with its altered perception of reality, takes over unchecked, it is difficult to build authentic relationships, since the objective and real premises of communication are lacking.

For her part, the Church can never be exempted from speaking the truth about humanity and the

* Leo XIII, Encyclical Letter *Rerum Novarum*, May 15, 1891, 9.

world, resorting whenever necessary to blunt language that may initially create misunderstanding. Yet truth can never be separated from charity, which always has at its root a concern for the life and well-being of every man and woman. Furthermore, from the Christian perspective, truth is not the affirmation of abstract and disembodied principles, but an encounter with the person of Christ himself, alive in the midst of the community of believers. Truth, then, does not create division, but rather enables us to confront all the more resolutely the challenges of our time, such as migration, the ethical use of artificial intelligence, and the protection of our beloved planet Earth. These are challenges that require commitment and cooperation on the part of all, since no one can think of facing them alone.

Dear Ambassadors, my ministry has begun in the heart of a Jubilee Year, devoted in a particular way to hope. It is a time of conversion and renewal and, above all, an opportunity to leave conflicts behind and embark on a new path, confident that, by working together, each of us in accordance with his or her own sensibilities and responsibilities can build a world in which everyone can lead an authentically human life in truth, justice, and peace. It is my hope that this will be the case everywhere, starting with those places that suffer most grievously, like Ukraine and the Holy Land. I thank you for all the work you are doing to build bridges between your countries and the Holy See, and I cordially impart my blessing to you, your families, and your peoples. Thank you! Thank you for all the work that you do!

Love and Unity

Homily for the Holy Mass
at the Beginning of the Pontificate

SAINT PETER'S SQUARE

SUNDAY, MAY 18, 2025

I greet all of you with a heart full of gratitude at the beginning of the ministry that has been entrusted to me. Saint Augustine wrote, Lord, "you have made us for yourself, and our heart is restless until it rests in you."*

In these days, we have experienced intense emotions. The death of Pope Francis filled our hearts with sadness. In those difficult hours, we felt like the crowds that the Gospel says were "like sheep without a shepherd" (Mt 9:36). Then, on Easter Sunday, we received his final blessing, and, in the light of the resurrection, we experienced the days that followed in the certainty that the Lord never abandons his people, but gathers them when they are scattered

* Saint Augustine of Hippo, *Confessions* I, 1,1.

and guards them "as a shepherd guards his flock" (Jer 31:10).

In this spirit of faith, the College of Cardinals met for the conclave. Coming from different backgrounds and experiences, we placed in God's hands our desire to elect the new Successor of Peter, the Bishop of Rome, a shepherd capable of preserving the rich heritage of the Christian faith and, at the same time, looking to the future, in order to confront the questions, concerns, and challenges of today's world. Accompanied by your prayers, we could feel the working of the Holy Spirit, who was able to bring us into harmony, like musical instruments, so that our heartstrings could vibrate in a single melody.

I was chosen, without any merit of my own, and now, with fear and trembling, I come to you as a brother, who desires to be the servant of your faith and your joy, walking with you on the path of God's love, for he wants us all to be united in one family.

Love and unity: These are the two dimensions of the mission entrusted to Peter by Jesus.

We see this in today's Gospel, which takes us to the Sea of Galilee, where Jesus began the mission he received from the Father: to be a "fisher" of humanity in order to draw it up from the waters of evil and death. Walking along the shore, he had called Peter and the other first disciples to be, like him, "fishers of men." Now, after the resurrection, it is up to them to carry on this mission, to cast their nets again and again, to bring the hope of the Gospel into the "waters" of the world, to sail the seas of life so that all may experience God's embrace.

How can Peter carry out this task? The Gospel tells us that it is possible only because his own life was touched by the infinite and unconditional love of God, even in the hour of his failure and denial. For this reason, when Jesus addresses Peter, the Gospel uses the Greek verb *agapáo*, which refers to the love that God has for us, to the offering of himself without reserve and without calculation. Whereas the verb used in Peter's response describes the love of friendship that we have for one another.

Consequently, when Jesus asks Peter, "Simon, son of John, do you love me more than these?" (Jn 21:16), he is referring to the love of the Father. It is as if Jesus said to him, "Only if you have known and experienced this love of God, which never fails, will you be able to feed my lambs. Only in the love of

God the Father will you be able to love your brothers and sisters with that same 'more,' that is, by offering your life for your brothers and sisters."

Peter is thus entrusted with the task of "loving more" and giving his life for the flock. The ministry of Peter is distinguished precisely by this self-sacrificing love, because the Church of Rome presides in charity and its true authority is the charity of Christ. It is never a question of capturing others by force, by religious propaganda, or by means of power. Instead, it is always and only a question of loving as Jesus did.

The Apostle Peter himself tells us that Jesus "is the stone that was rejected by you, the builders, and has become the cornerstone" (Acts 4:11). Moreover, if the rock is Christ, Peter must shepherd the flock without ever yielding to the temptation to be an autocrat, lording it over those entrusted to him (cf. 1 Pt 5:3). On the contrary, he is called to serve the faith of his brothers and sisters, and to walk alongside them, for all of us are "living stones" (1 Pt 2:5), called through our baptism to build God's house in fraternal communion, in the harmony of the Spirit, in the coexistence of diversity. In the words of Saint Augustine: "The Church consists of all those who are in harmony with their brothers and sisters and who love their neighbour."*

Brothers and sisters, I would like that our first great desire be for *a united Church, a sign of unity and communion, which becomes a leaven for a reconciled world.*

In this our time, we still see too much discord, too many wounds caused by hatred, violence, prejudice, the fear of difference, and an economic paradigm that exploits the Earth's resources and marginalizes the poorest. For our part, we want to be a small leaven of unity, communion, and fraternity within the world. We want to say to the world, with humility and joy: Look to Christ! Come closer to him! Welcome his word that enlightens and consoles! Listen to his offer of love and become his one family: *In the one Christ, we are one.* This is the path to follow together, among ourselves but also with our sister Christian churches, with those who follow other religious paths, with those who are searching for God, with all women and men of goodwill, in order to build a new world where peace reigns!

This is the missionary spirit that must animate

* Saint Augustine of Hippo, *Sermons*, 359, 9.

us—not closing ourselves off in our small groups, nor feeling superior to the world. We are called to offer God's love to everyone, in order to achieve that unity which does not cancel out differences but values the personal history of each person and the social and religious culture of every people.

Brothers and sisters, this is the hour for love! The heart of the Gospel is the love of God that makes us brothers and sisters. With my predecessor Leo XIII, we can ask ourselves today: If this criterion "were to prevail in the world, would not every conflict cease and peace return?"*

With the light and the strength of the Holy Spirit, let us build a Church founded on God's love, a sign of unity, a missionary Church that opens its arms to the world, proclaims the word, allows itself to be made "restless" by history, and becomes a leaven of harmony for humanity. Together, as one people, as brothers and sisters, let us walk toward God and love one another.

---

* Leo XIII, Encyclical Letter *Rerum Novarum*, May 15, 1891, 21.

In the One, Christ, We Are One

Address to Representatives of Other Churches and Ecclesial Communities, and Other Religions

CLEMENTINE HALL

MONDAY, MAY 19, 2025

One of the strong emphases of Pope Francis's pontificate was that of universal fraternity. In this regard the Holy Spirit really "urged" him to advance with great strides the initiatives already undertaken by previous Pontiffs, especially since Saint John XXIII. The Pope of *Fratelli Tutti* promoted both the ecumenical path and inter-religious dialogue. He did so above all by cultivating interpersonal relations, in such a way that, without taking anything away from ecclesial bonds, the human trait of the encounter was always valued. May God help us to treasure his witness!

My election has taken place during the year of the seventeen-hundredth anniversary of the First Ecumenical Council of Nicaea. That council represents a milestone in the formulation of the creed shared by all churches and ecclesial communities. While we are on the journey to reestablishing full communion among all Christians, we recognize that this unity can only be unity in faith. As Bishop of Rome, I consider one of my priorities to be that of seeking the reestablishment of full and visible communion among all those who profess the same faith in God the Father, the Son, and the Holy Spirit.

Indeed, unity has always been a constant concern of mine, as witnessed by the motto I chose for my episcopal ministry: *In Illo uno unum*, an expression of Saint Augustine of Hippo that reminds us how we too, although we are many, "in the One—that is Christ—we are one."* What is more, our communion is realized to the extent that we meet in the Lord Jesus. The more faithful and obedient we are to him, the more united we are among ourselves. We Christians, then, are all called to pray and work together to reach this goal, step by step, which is and remains the work of the Holy Spirit.

Aware, moreover, that synodality and ecumenism are closely linked, I would like to assure you of my

* Saint Augustine of Hippo, *Enarrationes in Psalmos*, 127, 3.

intention to continue Pope Francis's commitment to promoting the synodal nature of the Catholic Church and developing new and concrete forms for an ever stronger synodality in ecumenical relations.

Our common path can and must also be understood in the broad sense of involving everyone, in the spirit of human fraternity that I mentioned above. Now is the time for dialogue and building bridges. I am therefore pleased and grateful for the presence of representatives of other religious traditions, who share the search for God and his will, which is always and only the will of love and life for men and women and for all creatures.

You have witnessed the remarkable efforts made by Pope Francis in favor of interreligious dialogue. Through his words and actions, he opened new avenues of encounter, to promote "the culture of dialogue as the path; mutual collaboration as the code of conduct; reciprocal understanding as the method and standard."* I thank the Dicastery for Interreligious Dialogue for the essential role it plays in this

---

* Francis and Ahmad Al-Tayyeb, *A Document on Human Fraternity for World Peace and Living Together*, February 4, 2019.

patient work of encouraging meetings and concrete exchanges aimed at building relationships based on human fraternity.

In a special way I greet our Jewish and Muslim brothers and sisters. Because of the Jewish roots of Christianity, all Christians have a special relationship with Judaism. The conciliar declaration *Nostra Aetate*[*] emphasizes the greatness of the spiritual heritage shared by Christians and Jews, encouraging mutual knowledge and esteem.[†] The theological dialogue between Christians and Jews remains ever important and close to my heart. Even in these difficult times, marked by conflicts and misunderstandings, it is necessary to continue the momentum of this precious dialogue of ours.

Relations between the Catholic Church and Muslims have been marked by a growing commitment to dialogue and fraternity, fostered by esteem for these our brothers and sisters who "worship God, who is one, living and subsistent, merciful and almighty, the Creator of heaven and earth, who has

* Cf. Vatican II, Declaration *Nostra Aetate* on the Relation of the Church to Non-Christian Religions, October 28, 1965.

† Cf. ibid.

also spoken to humanity.'"* This approach, based on mutual respect and freedom of conscience, is a solid foundation for building bridges between our communities.

To all of you, representatives of other religious traditions, I express my gratitude for your participation in this meeting and for your contribution to peace. In a world wounded by violence and conflict, each of the communities represented here brings its own contribution of wisdom, compassion, and commitment to the good of humanity and the preservation of our common home. I am convinced that if we are in agreement, and free from ideological and political conditioning, we can be effective in saying "no" to war and "yes" to peace, "no" to the arms race and "yes" to disarmament, "no" to an economy that impoverishes peoples and the Earth and "yes" to integral development.

The witness of our fraternity, which I hope we will be able to show with effective gestures, will certainly contribute to building a more peaceful world,

* Vatican II, Declaration *Nostra Aetate* on the Relation of the Church to Non-Christian Religions, October 28, 1965, 3.

something that all men and women of goodwill desire in their hearts.

Dear friends, thank you again for your closeness. Let us ask for God's blessing in our hearts: May his infinite goodness and wisdom help us to live as his children and as brothers and sisters to each other, so that hope may grow in the world. I offer you my heartfelt gratitude.

Grace, Faith, and Justification

Homily for the Visit to the Tomb of Saint Paul

BASILICA OF SAINT PAUL OUTSIDE THE WALLS

TUESDAY, MAY 20, 2025

The passage of Scripture that we have just heard is the opening of a beautiful letter written by Saint Paul to the Christians of Rome. Its message revolves around three great themes: *grace*, *faith*, and *justification*. As we entrust the beginning of this new pontificate to the intercession of the Apostle of the Gentiles, let us reflect together on that message.

Saint Paul starts by saying that he received from God the *grace* of his vocation (cf. Rom 1:5). He acknowledges, in other words, that his encounter with Christ and his own ministry were the fruit of God's prior love, which called him to a new life while he was still far from the Gospel and was persecuting the Church. Saint Augustine, who was also a convert, spoke of the same experience in these words:

"How can we choose, unless we have first been chosen? We cannot love, unless someone has loved us first."* At the root of every vocation, God is present, in his mercy and his goodness, as generous as that of a mother (cf. Is 66:11–13) who nourishes her child with her own body for as long as the child is unable to feed itself.†

In the same passage, Paul also speaks of "the obedience of faith" (Rom 1:5), and here too he shares his own experience. When the Lord appeared to him on the road to Damascus (cf. Acts 9:1–30), he did not take away his freedom, but gave him the opportunity to make a decision, to choose an obedience that would prove costly and entail interior and exterior struggles, which Paul proved willing to face. Salvation does not come about by magic, but by a mysterious interplay of *grace* and *faith*, of God's prevenient love and of our trusting and free acceptance (cf. 2 Tm 1:12).

As we thank the Lord for the calling that changed Saul's life, let us ask him to enable us to respond in

* Saint Augustine of Hippo, *Sermons*, 34, 2.

† Cf. Saint Augustine of Hippo, *Enarrationes in Psalmos*, 130, 9.

the same way to his grace, and to become, ourselves, witnesses of the love "poured into our hearts through the Holy Spirit who has been given to us" (Rom 5:5). Let us ask the Lord for the grace to cultivate and spread his charity, and to become true neighbors to one another.* Let us compete in showing the love that, following his encounter with Christ, drove the former persecutor to become "all things to all people" (cf. 1 Cor 9:19–23), even to the point of martyrdom. In this way, for us as for Paul, the weakness of the flesh will show the power of faith in God that brings *justification* (cf. Rom 5:1–5).

For centuries, this basilica has been entrusted to the care of a Benedictine community. How can we fail to mention, then, as we speak of love as the source and driving force of the preaching of the Gospel, the insistent appeals of Saint Benedict, in his rule, to fraternal charity in the monastery and hospitality toward all.†

I would like to conclude, though, by recalling the words that, more than a thousand years later, another

* Cf. Francis, *Homily at Second Vespers of the Solemnity of the Conversion of Saint Paul*, January 25, 2024.

† Cf. Saint Benedict, *Rule*, cc. LIII, LXIII.

Benedict, Pope Benedict XVI, addressed to young people: "Dear friends," he said, "God loves us. This is the great truth of our life; it is what makes everything else meaningful." Indeed, "our life originates as part of a loving plan of God," and faith leads us to "open our hearts to this mystery of love and to live as men and women conscious of being loved by God."*

Here we see, in all its simplicity and uniqueness, the basis of every mission, including my own mission as the Successor of Peter and the heir to Paul's apostolic zeal. May the Lord grant me the grace to respond faithfully to his call.

* Benedict XVI, *Homily at the Prayer Vigil with Young People*, August 20, 2011.

Builders of Unity

Meeting with Employees of the Holy See and the Vatican City State

AUDIENCE HALL

SATURDAY, MAY 24, 2025

Thank you! When the applause lasts longer than the address, I will have to make a longer address! So . . . be careful! Thank you! Thank you!

This first meeting of ours is certainly not the moment to make keynote speeches, but rather it is an opportunity for me to thank you for the service you carry out, and this service that I have, so to speak, "inherited" from my predecessors. Thank you indeed. Yes, as you know, I arrived only two years ago, when our beloved Pope Francis appointed me as Prefect of the Dicastery for Bishops. Then I left the diocese of Chiclayo, in Peru, and came to work here. What a change! And now, then . . . What can I say? Only what Simon Peter said to Jesus on Lake Tiberias: "Lord, you know everything; you know that I love you" (Jn 21:17).

Popes pass, the curia remains. This applies to every particular church, for the episcopal curias. And it also applies to the Curia of the Bishop of Rome. The curia is the institution that preserves and transmits the historical memory of a church, of the ministry of its bishops. This is very important. Memory is an essential element in a living organism. It is not only directed to the past, but nourishes the present and guides the future. Without memory, the path is lost, it loses its sense of direction.

Here, dear friends, is the first thought I would like to share with you: to work in the Roman Curia means to contribute to keeping the memory of the Apostolic See alive, in the vital sense I have just mentioned, so that the Pope's ministry may be implemented in the best way. And, by analogy, this can also be said of the services of the Vatican City State.

Then, there is another aspect I would like to recall, complementary to that of memory, that is the *missionary* dimension of the Church and of every institution linked to the Petrine ministry. This was insisted upon a great deal by Pope Francis who, consistently with the project laid out in the apostolic exhortation *Evangelii Gaudium*, reformed the Roman Curia from the perspective of evangelization, with the apostolic constitution *Praedicate Evangelium*. And he did this by following in the footsteps of his predecessors, especially Saint Paul VI and Saint John Paul II.

As I think you know, the experience of mission forms part of my life, and not only as a baptized person, as for all us Christians, but because as an Augustinian religious I was a missionary in Peru, and in the midst of the Peruvian people my pastoral vocation matured. I will never be able to thank the Lord enough for this gift! Then, the call to serve the Church here in the Roman Curia was a new mission, which I shared with you during these past two years. And still I continue it and will continue it, as long as God wills, in this service that has been entrusted to me.

Therefore, I repeat to you what I said in my first greeting, in the evening of May 8: "Together, we must look for ways to be a missionary Church, a Church that builds bridges and encourages dialogue, a Church ever open to welcoming . . . with open arms, all those who are in need of our charity, our presence, our readiness to dialogue and our love."* These words were addressed to the Church of Rome. And now I repeat them, thinking of the mission of this Church toward all the churches and the entire world, of serving communion, unity, in charity and in truth. The Lord gave this task to Peter and his successors, and you all collaborate in different ways in this great task. Each one of you gives your contribution, carrying out your daily work with commitment and also with faith, because faith and prayer are like salt for food; they impart flavor.

If, then, we must all cooperate in the great cause of unity and love, let us seek to do so first of all with our behavior in everyday situations, starting also from the work environment. Each person can be a builder of unity with his attitudes toward colleagues, overcoming inevitable misunderstandings with patience, with humility, putting himself in the shoes of others, avoiding prejudices, and also with a good dose of humor, as Pope Francis taught us.

---

* Leo XIV, Apostolic Blessing *Urbi et Orbi*, May 8, 2025.

Dear brothers and sisters, thank you again from the bottom of my heart! We are in the month of May: Let us invoke the Virgin Mary together, so that she may bless the Roman Curia and Vatican City, and also your families, especially children, the elderly, and the sick and suffering.

Listen, Understand, Remember

Homily for the Mass for the Possession of the Chair of the Bishop of Rome

LATERAN BASILICA

SUNDAY, MAY 25, 2025

The Church of Rome is heir to a great history, grounded in the witness of Peter, Paul, and countless martyrs, and it has a unique mission, as we see from the inscription on the façade of this cathedral: to be *Mater omnium Ecclesiarum*, Mother of all the Churches.

Pope Francis frequently encouraged us to reflect on the maternal dimension of the Church and her defining qualities of tenderness, self-sacrifice, and the capacity to listen.* Those qualities enable her not only to assist others but often to anticipate their needs and expectations before they are even expressed. We hope that those qualities will be in-

* Cf. Francis, Apostolic Exhortation *Evangelii Gaudium* on the Proclamation of the Gospel in Today's World, November 24, 2013, 46–49, 139–141; and *Catechesis*, January 13, 2016.

creasingly present in the people of God everywhere, including here, in our great diocesan family: in the faithful, in pastors, and, first of all, in myself. The readings we have heard can help us to reflect on these qualities.

The Acts of the Apostles (cf. 15:1–2, 22–29) in particular describe how the early Christian community faced the challenge of opening to the pagan world in its preaching of the Gospel. This was no easy matter; it called for much patience and mutual listening. This was the case in the community in Antioch, where the brethren, through dialogue—and even disagreements—resolved the question together. Paul and Barnabas then went up to Jerusalem. They did not settle the question on their own: They wanted to be in communion with the Mother Church and so they went there with humility.

In Jerusalem, they found Peter and the apostles, who were prepared to listen to them. This was the beginning of a dialogue that, in the end, led to the right decision. Recognizing the difficulties of the new converts, they agreed not to impose excessive burdens on them, but rather to insist only on what was essential (cf. Acts 15:28–29). In this way, what might have seemed a problem became for everyone an opportunity for reflection and growth.

The biblical text, however, tells us something else, beyond the rich and interesting human dynamics of the event.

We see this in the words used by the brethren in Jerusalem to communicate their decisions to those in Antioch. They wrote, "For it has seemed good to the Holy Spirit and to us" (Acts 15:28). In other words, they emphasized that the most important part of the entire event was listening to God's voice, which made everything else possible. In this way, they remind us that communion is built primarily "on our knees," through prayer and constant commitment to conversion. For only in this way can each of us hear within the voice of the Spirit crying out, "Abba! Father!" (Gal 4:6), and then, as a result, listen to and understand others as our brothers and sisters.

The Gospel reaffirms this point (cf. Jn 14:23–29). It assures us that we are not alone in making our decisions in life. The Spirit sustains us and shows us the way to follow, "teaching" us and "reminding" us of all that Jesus said to us (cf. Jn 14:26).

First, the Spirit *teaches* us the Lord's words by impressing them deep within us, written, as the biblical image would have it, no longer on tablets of stone but in our hearts (cf. Jer 31:33). This gift helps us grow and become "a letter of Christ" (2 Cor 3:3) for one another. Naturally, the more we let ourselves be convinced and transformed by the Gospel—allowing the power of the Spirit to purify our hearts, to make our words straightforward, our desires honest and clear, and our actions generous—the more capable we are of proclaiming its message.

Here, the other verb comes into play: We *remember*, that is, we reflect in our hearts upon what we have experienced and learned, in order to understand more fully its meaning and to savor its beauty.

I think in this regard of the challenging process of listening that the Diocese of Rome has undertaken in these years, a process carried out at various levels: listening to the world around us to respond to its challenges, and listening within our communities to understand needs and to propose sage and prophetic initiatives of evangelization and charity. This has been a challenging, ongoing journey meant to embrace a very rich and complex reality. Yet it is worthy of the history of this local Church, which has shown, time and again, that it is able to "think big," unafraid to embark on bold projects and to confront new and challenging scenarios.

This is evident in the great efforts and many initiatives that the diocese has made to welcome and provide for the needs of pilgrims during the present Jubilee. Thank you! These have made the city of Rome appear to visitors, some of whom have traveled from far away, as a wide, open, and welcoming home, and above all as a place of deep faith.

For my part, I would like to express my firm desire to contribute to this great ongoing process by listening to everyone as much as possible, in order to learn, understand, and decide things together, as Saint Augustine would say, "as a Christian with you and a Bishop for you."* I would also ask you to support me in prayer and charity, mindful of the words of Saint Leo the Great: "All the good we do in the exercise of our ministry is the work of Christ and not our own, for we can do nothing without him. Yet we glory in

* Saint Augustine of Hippo, *Sermons*, 340, 1.

him, from whom all the effectiveness of our work is derived."*

Let me conclude by adding the words with which Blessed John Paul I, whose joyful and serene face had already earned him the nickname of "the smiling Pope," greeted his new diocesan family on September 23, 1978. "Saint Pius X," he said, "upon entering Venice as patriarch, exclaimed in Saint Mark's: 'What would become of me, dear Venetians, if I did not love you?' I would say something similar to you Romans: I assure you that I love you, that I desire only to enter into your service and to place my own poor abilities, the little I have and am, at the service of all."†

I too express my affection for you and my desire to share with you, on our journey together, our joys and sorrows, our struggles and hopes. I too offer you "the little I have and am," entrusting it to the intercession of Saints Peter and Paul and of all those other brothers and sisters of ours whose holiness has illuminated the history of this Church and the streets of this city. May the Virgin Mary accompany us and intercede for us.

* Pope Leo I, *Sermon* 5, *De Natali Ipsius*, 4.

† John Paul I, *Homily for the Taking of Possession of the Chair of the Bishop of Rome*, September 23, 1978.

[Pope Leo XIV's words spoken from the central loggia of the Basilica of Saint John Lateran for the blessing of the city of Rome at the conclusion of the eucharistic celebration.] Peace be with you!

Dear brothers and sisters, community of Rome, it gives me great pleasure to be here with you this evening, in this liturgical act in which we have celebrated my inauguration as your new Bishop of Rome. Thank you all!

Let us live our faith, especially during this Jubilee Year, in search of hope, but seeking to be ourselves the witness that offers hope to the world. A world that suffers a great deal of pain due to wars, violence, and poverty! But the Lord asks us as Christians always to be this living witness. To live our faith, feeling in our heart that Jesus Christ is present and to know that he always accompanies us on our journey.

Thank you for walking together! Let us all walk together! Always count on me, as a Christian with you and bishop for you. Thank you all!

To Liberate, Not to Possess

Homily for the Holy Mass with Presbyteral Ordinations
Feast of the Visitation of the Blessed Virgin Mary

SAINT PETER'S BASILICA

SATURDAY, MAY 31, 2025

Today is a day of great joy for the Church, for each of you, ordination candidates, for your families and friends, and for your traveling companions during your years of formation. As the Rite of Ordination highlights in several passages, the relationship between what we are celebrating today and the people of God is fundamental. The depth, breadth, and even duration of the divine joy that we now share are directly proportional to the bonds that exist and will grow between you, candidates, and the people from whom you hail, whom you continue to be a part of, and to whom you will be sent. I will linger on this aspect, bearing in mind that priests' identities are rooted in the union with Christ, the Eternal and High Priest.

We are the people of God. The Second Vatican

Council made this awareness clearer, almost anticipating a time in which affiliations would grow weaker, and the awareness of God more rarefied. You bear witness to the fact that God has not grown tired of bringing his children together, diverse though they may be, and of forming them into a dynamic unity. It is not an impulsive action, but rather the gentle breeze that restored hope to the prophet Elijah when he was in despair (cf. 1 Kgs 19:12). God's joy is not loud, but it truly changes history and brings us closer to one another. An icon of this mystery is the Visitation, which the Church contemplates on the last day of May. The Magnificat, the song of a people visited by grace, emerges from the encounter between the Virgin Mary and her cousin Elizabeth.

The readings we have just read also help us interpret what is happening among us. First, in the Gospel, Jesus does not appear crushed by his imminent death, nor by the bonds that were broken or left incomplete. On the contrary, the Holy Spirit strengthens these threatened bonds. In prayer, they become stronger than death. Instead of thinking about his own personal destiny, Jesus puts the bonds that he built "down here" into the Father's hands. We are part of them! Indeed, the Gospel came to us through these relationships—bonds that the world can wear down, but not destroy.

Dear ordinands, imitate Jesus! Being of God—servants of God, people of God—connects us to the Earth: not to an ideal world, but to the real one. Like Jesus, you meet real people whom the Father places on your path. Consecrate yourselves to them, without separating, isolating, or turning the gift you received into a privilege. Pope Francis warned us about this many times because self-centeredness extinguishes the fire of the missionary spirit.

The Church is outgoing like the life, passion, death, and resurrection of Jesus. In every Eucharist you make his words your own: It is "for you and for all." No one has ever seen God. He turned to us; he came out of himself. The Son became the exegesis, the living story. And he gave us the power to become children of God. Do not seek, let us not seek, any other power!

May the gesture of laying on of the hands, with which Jesus welcomed children and healed the sick, renew the liberating power of his messianic ministry, within you. In the Acts of the Apostles, that gesture we will soon repeat is the invocation of the Spirit, creator. In this way, the Kingdom of God now unites your personal freedoms, that are ready to go beyond, engaging your intelligence and your youthful strength in the jubilee mission that Jesus entrusted to his Church.

In his greeting to the elders of the community of Ephesus, which we heard in the first reading, Paul conveys the secret of every mission: "The Holy Spirit has made you guardians" (Acts 20:28). Not masters, but guardians. The mission is Jesus. He is risen—thus, he is living and he precedes us. None of us is called to substitute him. The day of the ascension teaches us about his invisible presence. He trusts us, he makes room for us; he even went so far as to say, "It is better for you that I go" (Jn 16:7). By involving you in the mission, dear ordinands, we bishops make room for you too. And you make room for the faithful and for every creature to whom the Risen One is close and in whom he loves to visit and surprise us. The people of God are more numerous than we see. Let us not define their boundaries.

I would like to highlight another part of the passage from Saint Paul, from his moving farewell discourse. In fact it comes before all the other words. He can say, "You know how I lived among you the whole time" (Acts 20:18). Let us keep this expression clearly in our hearts and minds! "You know how I lived": the transparency of life. Lives that are known, legible lives, credible lives! We live among the people of God, so that we may stand before them as credible witnesses.

Together, then, we will rebuild the credibility of a wounded Church, sent to a wounded humanity, within a wounded creation. We are not yet perfect, but it is necessary that we be credible.

The Risen Jesus shows us his wounds, and although they are a sign of humanity's rejection, he forgives us and sends us on our way. Let us not forget this! He breathes on us today too (cf. Jn 20:22), and he makes us ministers of hope. "From now on, therefore, we regard no one from a human point of view" (2 Cor 5:16). Everything that seems lost and broken to us, now appears in the sign of reconciliation.

"For the love of Christ controls us," dear brothers and sisters! It is a "control" that is liberating and enables us to not control anyone. To liberate, not to possess. We are God's. There is no greater wealth to be appreciated and shared. It is the only wealth that, when shared, is multiplied. Together we want to bring it to the world that God loved so much that he gave his only Son (cf. Jn 3:16).

Thus, the life given by these brothers, who will soon be ordained priests, is full of meaning. We thank them and we thank God who called them to the service of an all-priestly people. Indeed, together we bridge heaven and earth. This shared priesthood that lifts up the lowly, binds generations, and allows us to be called blessed (cf. Lk 1:48, 52) shines forth in Mary, Mother of the Church. May she, Our Lady of Trust and Mother of Hope, intercede for us.

We Are One in Our Savior

Homily for the Mass for the Jubilee of Families, Children, Grandparents, and the Elderly

ST. PETER'S SQUARE

SUNDAY, JUNE 1, 2025

The Gospel we have just heard shows us Jesus, at the Last Supper, praying on our behalf (cf. Jn 17:20). The Word of God, made man, as he nears the end of his earthly life, thinks of us, his brothers and sisters, and becomes a blessing, a prayer of petition and praise to the Father, in the power of the Holy Spirit. As we ourselves, full of wonder and trust, enter into Jesus's prayer, we become, thanks to his love, part of a great plan that concerns all of humanity.

Christ prays that we may "all be one" (Jn 17:21). This is the greatest good that we can desire, for this universal union brings about among his creatures the eternal communion of love that is God himself: the Father who gives life, the Son who receives it, and the Spirit who shares it.

The Lord does not want us, in this unity, to be a nameless and faceless crowd. He wants us to be one: "As you, Father, are in me and I am in you, may they also be in us" (Jn 17:21). The unity for which Jesus prays is thus a communion grounded in the same love with which God loves, which brings life and salvation into the world. As such, it is firstly a *gift* that Jesus comes to bring. From his human heart, the Son of God prays to the Father in these words: "I in them and you in me, that they may become completely one, so that the world may know that you have sent me and have loved them even as you have loved me" (Jn 17:23).

Let us listen with amazement to these words. Jesus is telling us that God loves us as he loves himself. The Father does not love us any less than he loves his only begotten Son. In other words, with an infinite love. God does not love less, because he loves first, from the very beginning! Christ himself bears witness to this when he says to the Father, "You loved me before the foundation of the world" (Jn 17:24). And so it is: In his mercy, God has always desired to draw all people to himself. It is his life, bestowed upon us in Christ, that makes us one, uniting us with one another.

Listening to this Gospel today, during the Jubilee of Families, Children, Grandparents, and the Elderly, fills us with joy.

Dear friends, we received life before we ever desired it. As Pope Francis said, "All of us are sons and daughters, but none of us chose to be born."* Not only that. As soon as we were born, we needed others in order to live; left to ourselves, we would not have survived. Someone else saved us by caring for us in body and spirit. All of us are alive today thanks to a relationship, a free and freeing relationship of human kindness and mutual care.

That human kindness is sometimes betrayed. As, for example, whenever freedom is invoked not to give life, but to take it away, not to help, but to hurt. Yet even in the face of the evil that opposes and takes life, Jesus continues to pray to the Father for us. His prayer acts as a balm for our wounds; it speaks to us of forgiveness and reconciliation. That prayer makes fully meaningful our experience of love for one another as parents, grandparents, sons, and daughters. That is what we want to proclaim to the

* Francis, *Angelus*, January 1, 2025.

world: We are here in order to be "one" as the Lord wants us to be "one," in our families and in those places where we live, work, and study. Different, yet one; many, yet one—always, in every situation and at every stage of life.

Dear friends, if we love one another in this way, grounded in Christ, who is "the Alpha and the Omega," "the beginning and the end" (Rv 22:13), we will be a sign of peace for everyone, in society and the world. Let us not forget: Families are the cradle of the future of humanity.

In recent decades, we have received a sign that fills us with joy but also makes us think. It is the fact that several spouses have been beatified and canonized, not separately, but as married couples. I think of Louis and Zélie Martin, the parents of Saint Thérèse of the Child Jesus; and of Blessed Luigi and Maria Beltrame Quattrocchi, who raised a family in Rome in the past century. And let us not forget the Ulma family from Poland: parents and children, united in love and martyrdom. I said that this is a sign that makes us think. By pointing to them as exemplary witnesses of married life, the Church tells us that today's world needs the marriage covenant in order to know and accept God's love and to defeat, thanks to its unifying and reconciling power, the forces that break down relationships and societies.

For this reason, with a heart filled with gratitude and hope, I would remind all married couples that marriage is not an ideal but the measure of true love between a man and a woman: a love that is total, faithful, and fruitful.* This love makes you one flesh and enables you, in the image of God, to bestow the gift of life.

I encourage you, then, to be examples of integrity to your children, acting as you want them to act, educating them in freedom through obedience, always seeing the good in them and finding ways to nurture it. And you, dear children, show gratitude to your parents. To say "thank you" each day for the gift of life and for all that comes with it is the first way to honor your father and your mother (cf. Ex 20:12). Finally, dear grandparents and elderly people, I recommend that you watch over your loved ones with wisdom and compassion, and with the humility and patience that come with age.

---

* Cf. Paul VI, Encyclical Letter *Humanae Vitae*, July 25, 1968, 9.

In the family, faith is handed on together with life, generation after generation. It is shared like food at the family table and like the love in our hearts. In this way, families become privileged places in which to encounter Jesus, who loves us and desires our good, always.

Let me add one last thing. The prayer of the Son of God, which gives us hope on our journey, also reminds us that one day we will all be *uno unum*:* one in the one Savior, embraced by the eternal love of God. Not only us, but also our fathers, mothers, grandmothers, grandfathers, brothers, sisters, and children who have already gone before us into the light of his eternal Pasch, and whose presence we feel here, together with us, in this moment of celebration.

* Cf. Saint Augustine of Hippo, *Enarrationes in Psalmos*, 127.

Incarnation and Catholicity

Address to Superiors and Officials of the Secretariat of State

CLEMENTINE HALL

THURSDAY, JUNE 5, 2025

I am pleased to be here with you, who offer a precious service to the life of the Church by helping to carry out the mission entrusted to me. Indeed, as *Praedicate Evangelium* affirms, "The Secretariat of State, as the Papal Secretariat, provides close assistance to the Roman Pontiff in the exercise of his supreme mission."*

I am comforted by the knowledge that I am not alone and that I can share the responsibility of my universal ministry with you.

This is not in the prepared text, but I can say with great sincerity that in these few weeks—a month has not even passed yet since beginning my Petrine

---

* Cf. Francis, Apostolic Constitution *Praedicate Evangelium* on the Roman Curia and Its Service to the Church in the World, March 19, 2022, Art. 44.

ministry—it is evident to me that the Pope cannot work alone. There is great necessity to rely on the assistance of many people in the Holy See, and in a special way on all of you in the Secretariat of State. I offer my heartfelt thanks!

The history of this institution dates back, as we know, to the end of the fifteenth century. Over time, it has taken on an increasingly universal character and has grown considerably, acquiring additional tasks in response to emerging needs both within the Church and in relations with states and international organizations. Currently, almost half of you are lay faithful. And there are more than fifty women, both lay and religious.

This development means that, today, the Secretariat of State itself reflects the face of the Church. It is a large community working alongside the Pope: Together we share the questions, difficulties, challenges, and hopes of the People of God throughout the world. In doing so, we always express two essential dimensions: *incarnation* and *catholicity*.

We are incarnate in time and history since God chose the human condition and the languages of humanity. The Church, therefore, is called to follow the same path, in order that the joy of the Gospel may reach everyone, mediated through today's cultures and languages. At the same time, we always seek to maintain a catholic, universal outlook that allows us to appreciate different cultures and sensibilities. In this way, we can be a driving force committed to building communion between the Church of Rome and the local churches, as well as friendly relationships in the international community.

In recent decades, these two dimensions—being incarnate in time and having a universal outlook—have become increasingly constitutive of the Curia's work. We have been guided along this path by the reform of the Roman Curia carried out by Saint Paul VI who, inspired by the vision of the Second Vatican Council, strongly felt the urgency for the Church to be attentive to the challenges of history, taking into account "the rapid pace of modern life" and "the changed conditions of our times."* At the same time, he reaffirmed the need for a service that

---

* Paul VI, Apostolic Constitution *Regimini Ecclesiae Universi—The Roman Curia,* August 15, 1967.

expresses the catholicity of the Church, and to this end he decreed that "those present in the Apostolic See to govern it, should be called from all parts of the world."*

Incarnation reminds us, then, of the concreteness of reality and the specific, particular issues dealt with by the various curial institutions. At the same time, *universality* evokes the mystery of the multi-faceted unity of the Church and requires a subsequent effort of synthesis to assist the Pope's mission. It is precisely the Secretariat of State that offers this service of unification and synthesis. Indeed, Paul VI—well-versed in the Roman Curia—chose to restructure this office, effectively designating it as a point of connection, and thus establishing its fundamental role of coordinating the other dicasteries and institutions of the Apostolic See.

The recent apostolic constitution *Praedicate Evangelium* speaks of the coordinating role of the Secretariat of State as one of the many responsibilities entrusted to the Section for General Affairs, under

* Paul VI, Apostolic Constitution *Regimini Ecclesiae Univers—The Roman Curia,* August 15, 1967.

the direction of the Substitute with the assistance of the Assessor.* Along with the Section for General Affairs, the constitution also includes the Section for Relations with States and International Organizations, which is directed by the secretary with the help of two undersecretaries. This section is responsible, particularly in this delicate moment of history, for the diplomatic and political relations of the Holy See with states and other subjects of international law. The Section for Diplomatic Personnel, with its secretary and undersecretary, is tasked for its part with assisting pontifical representations and the members of the Diplomatic Corps in Rome and throughout the world.

I know that these tasks are very demanding and, at times, may not be well-understood. This is why I wish to express my closeness to you and, above all, my heartfelt gratitude. Thank you for the skills you place at the service of the Church, for your work—which almost always goes unnoticed—and for the evangelical spirit that inspires it. And allow me, as a result of my gratitude, to make an appeal, refer-

* Cf. Francis, *Praedicate Evangelium*, 45–46.

ring once again to Saint Paul VI: Let this place not be clouded by ambition or rivalry; instead, let it be a true community of faith and charity, of "brothers and sisters, and children of the Pope," who give themselves generously for the good of the Church.*

I entrust you all to the intercession of the Blessed Virgin Mary, Mother of the Church. I thank you because I know that you pray for me—I hope!—every day, and I warmly bless each of you, your loved ones, and your work. Thank you!

* Paul VI, *Address to the Roman Curia*, September 21, 1963.

Walking Alongside One Another

Homily for the Vigil of Pentecost

ST. PETER'S SQUARE

SATURDAY, JUNE 7, 2025

The Creator Spirit, whom we invoked in the hymn—*Veni Creator Spiritus*—is the Spirit who descended upon Jesus as the quiet driving force of his mission: "The Spirit of the Lord is upon me" (Lk 4:18). When we ask the Spirit to enlighten our minds, to multiply our languages, to awaken our senses, to instill love, to strengthen our bodies, and to grant us peace, we become open to God's Kingdom. This is, according to the Gospel, the meaning of conversion. It is a "turning toward" the Kingdom already close at hand.

In Jesus we see, and from Jesus we hear, how everything changes because God is king, God is close to us. On this vigil of Pentecost, we are deeply aware of this closeness of God, of his Spirit who joins our lives to that of Jesus. We are caught up in the new things that God brings about, so that his desire for the fullness of life will prevail over the power of death.

"He has anointed me to preach good news to the poor. He has sent me to proclaim release to the captives and recovering of sight to the blind, to set at liberty those who are oppressed, to proclaim the acceptable year of the Lord" (Lk 4:18–19). Here tonight, we sense the fragrance of the chrism with which our foreheads have been anointed. Dear brothers and sisters, baptism and confirmation united us to Jesus's mission of making all things new, to the Kingdom of God. Just as love enables us to sense the presence of a loved one, so tonight we sense in one another the fragrance of Christ. This is a mystery; it amazes us and it leads us to reflect.

At Pentecost, Mary, the apostles, and the disciples with them received a Spirit of unity, which forever grounded in the one Lord Jesus Christ all their diversity. Theirs were not multiple missions, but a single mission. They were no longer introverted and quarreling with one another, but outgoing and radiant with joy. Saint Peter's Square, with its wide-open and welcoming embrace, magnificently expresses the communion of the Church that each of you has experienced in your various associations and communities, many of which are the fruit of the Second Vatican Council.

On the evening of my election, moved as I looked out at the people of God gathered here, I spoke of *synodality*, a word that aptly expresses how the Spirit shapes the Church. That word begins with the Greek word *syn*—meaning "with"—which speaks of the secret of God's life. God is not solitary. God, as Father, Son, and Holy Spirit, is a "with" in himself, and God with us. At the same time, the word *synodality* speaks to us of a road ahead—*hodós*—for where there is the Spirit, there is movement, a journey to be made. We are a people on the move. This does not set us apart but unites us to humanity like the yeast in a mass of dough, which causes it to rise. The year of the Lord's grace, reflected in the current Jubilee, has this fermentation within it. In a divided and troubled world, the Holy Spirit teaches us to walk together in unity. The Earth will rest, justice will prevail, the poor will rejoice, and peace will return, once we no longer act as predators but as pilgrims. No longer each of us for ourselves, but walking alongside one another. Not greedily exploiting this world, but cultivating it and protecting it, as the encyclical *Laudato Si'* has taught us.*

Dear friends, God created the world so that we might all live as one. *Synodality* is the ecclesial name for this. It demands that we each recognize our own poverty and our riches, that we feel part of a greater whole, apart from which everything withers, even the most original and unique of charisms. Think about it. All creation exists solely in the form of coexistence, sometimes dangerous, yet always interconnected.† And what we call "history" only takes place as coexistence, living together, however contentiously, but always together. The opposite is lethal, but sadly, we are witnessing this daily. May your meetings and your communities, then, be training grounds of fraternity and sharing, not merely meeting places, but centers of spirituality. The Spirit of Jesus changes the world because he changes hearts. The Spirit inspires the contemplative dimension of life that rejects self-assertion, complaining, rivalry, and the temptation to

* Cf. Francis, Encyclical Letter *Laudato Si'* on Care for Our Common Home, May 24, 2015.

† Cf. ibid, 16, 117.

control consciences and resources. The Lord is the Spirit, and where the Spirit of the Lord is, there is freedom (cf. 2 Cor 3:17). An authentic spirituality thus commits us to integral human development, to making Jesus's words a reality in our lives. When this happens, there is always joy: joy and hope.

Evangelization, dear brothers and sisters, is not our attempt to conquer the world, but the infinite grace that radiates from lives transformed by the Kingdom of God. It is the way of the beatitudes, a path that we tread together, between the "already" and the "not yet," hungering and thirsting for justice, poor in spirit, merciful, meek, pure of heart, men and women of peace. Jesus himself chose this path: To follow it, we have no need of powerful patrons, worldly compromises, or emotional strategies. Evangelization is always God's work. If at times it takes place through us, it is thanks to the bonds that it makes possible. So be deeply attached to each of the particular churches and parish communities in which you cultivate and exercise your charisms. Together with the bishops and in cooperation with all the other members of the Body of Christ, all of us will then work together harmoniously as one. The challenges facing humanity will be less frightening, the future will be less dark, and discernment will be less complicated if together we obey the Holy Spirit! May Mary, Queen of the Apostles and Mother of the Church, intercede for us.

The Spirit Opens Borders

Homily for the Holy Mass on the Solemnity of Pentecost, Jubilee of Movements, Associations, and New Communities

ST. PETER'S SQUARE

SUNDAY, JUNE 8, 2025

"The day has dawned upon us when . . . , glorified by his ascension into heaven following his resurrection, the Lord Jesus Christ sent the Holy Spirit."* Today, too, what took place in the Upper Room takes place anew in our midst. Like a mighty wind that overtakes us, like a crash that startles us, like a fire that illuminates us, the gift of the Holy Spirit descends upon us (cf. Acts 2:1–11).

As we heard in the first reading, the Spirit accomplished something extraordinary in the lives of the apostles. Following Jesus's death, they had retreated behind closed doors, in fear and sadness. Now they receive a new way of seeing things, an interior un-

* Saint Augustine of Hippo, *Sermons*, 271, 1.

derstanding that helps them to interpret the events that occurred and to experience intimately the presence of the Risen Lord. The Holy Spirit overcomes their fear, shatters their inner chains, heals their wounds, anoints them with strength, and grants them the courage to go out to all and to proclaim God's mighty works.

The reading from the Acts of the Apostles tells us that in Jerusalem at that time there was a multitude of people from various backgrounds, yet "each one heard them speaking in his own native tongue" (Acts 2:6). In a word, at Pentecost, *the doors of the Upper Room were opened* because *the Spirit opens borders.* As Benedict XVI explained:

> The Holy Spirit bestows understanding. The Spirit overcomes the "breach" that began in Babel, the confusion of mind and heart that sets us one against the other. The Spirit opens borders. . . . The Church must always become anew what she already is. She must open the borders between peoples and break down the barriers between class and race. In her, there cannot be those who are neglected or

> disdained. In the Church there are only free men and women, brothers and sisters of Jesus Christ.*

Here we have an eloquent image of Pentecost, one that I would like to pause for a moment and reflect upon with you.

The Spirit opens borders, first of all, in our hearts. He is the gift that opens our lives to love. His presence breaks down our hardness of heart, our narrowness of mind, our selfishness, the fears that enchain us, and the narcissism that makes us think only of ourselves. The Holy Spirit comes to challenge us, to make us confront the possibility that our lives are shriveling up, trapped in the vortex of individualism. Sadly, oddly enough, in a world of burgeoning "social" media, we risk being ever more alone. Constantly connected, yet incapable of "networking." Always immersed in a crowd, yet confused and solitary travelers.

The Spirit of God allows us to find a new way of approaching and experiencing life. He puts us in touch with our inmost self, beneath all the masks we

* Benedict XVI, *Homily for Pentecost*, May 15, 2005.

wear. He leads us to an encounter with the Lord by teaching us to experience the joy that is his gift. He convinces us, as we just heard in Jesus's words, that only by abiding in love will we receive the strength to remain faithful to his word and to let it transform us. The Spirit opens our interior borders, so that our lives can become places of welcome and refreshment.

The Spirit also opens borders in our relationships with others. Jesus tells us that this gift is the love between him and the Father that comes to dwell within us. We then become capable of opening our hearts to our brothers and sisters, overcoming our rigidity, moving beyond our fear of those who are different, and mastering the passions that stir within. The Spirit also transforms those deeper, hidden dangers that disturb our relationships, like suspicion, prejudice, or the desire to manipulate others. I think too, with great pain, of those cases where relationships are marked by an unhealthy desire for domination, an attitude that often leads to violence, as is shown, tragically, by numerous recent cases of femicide.

The Holy Spirit, on the other hand, brings to maturity within us the fruits that enable us to cultivate good and healthy relationships: "love, joy, peace, patience, kindness, generosity, faithfulness, gentleness and self-control" (Gal 5:22). In this way, the Spirit broadens the borders of our relationships and opens us to the joy of fraternity. This is also a critical yardstick for the Church. For we are truly the Church of the Risen Lord and disciples of Pentecost if there are no borders or divisions among us; if we are able to dialogue and accept one another in the Church, and to reconcile our diversities; and if, as Church, we become a welcoming and hospitable place for all.

Finally, *the Spirit also opens borders between peoples*. At Pentecost, the apostles spoke the languages of those they met, and the confusion of Babel was finally resolved by the harmony brought about by the Spirit. Whenever God's "breath" unites our hearts and makes us view others as our brothers and sisters, differences no longer become an occasion for division and conflict but rather a shared patrimony from which we can all draw, and which sets us all on a journey together, in fraternity.

The Spirit breaks down barriers and tears down the walls of indifference and hatred because he teaches us all things and reminds us of Jesus's words (cf. Jn 14:26). He teaches us, reminds us, and writes in our hearts before all else the commandment of love that the Lord has made the center and summit of everything. Where there is love, there is no room for prejudice, for "security" zones separating us from our neighbors, for the exclusionary mindset that, tragically, we now see emerging also in political nationalisms.

It was on the feast of Pentecost that Pope Francis observed: "In our world today, there is so much discord, such great division. We are all 'connected,' yet find ourselves disconnected from one another, anesthetized by indifference and overwhelmed by solitude."* The wars plaguing our world are a tragic sign of this. Let us invoke the Spirit of love and peace, that he may open borders, break down walls, dispel hatred, and help us to live as children of our one Father who is in heaven.

Brothers and sisters, Pentecost renews the Church and the world! May the strong wind of the Spirit come upon us and within us, open the borders of our hearts, grant us the grace of encounter with God, en-

* Francis, *Homily for Pentecost*, May 28, 2023.

large the horizons of our love, and sustain our efforts to build a world in which peace reigns.

May Mary Most Holy, Woman of Pentecost, Virgin visited by the Spirit, Mother full of grace, accompany us and intercede for us.

A Church Ever More Fruitful in the Spirit

Homily for the Mass
for the Jubilee of the Holy See
Blessed Virgin Mary Mother of the Church

SAINT PETER'S BASILICA

MONDAY, JUNE 9, 2025

Today we have the joy and grace of celebrating the Jubilee of the Holy See on the liturgical feast day of Mary, Mother of the Church. This happy coincidence is a source of light and inner inspiration in the Holy Spirit, who yesterday, on Pentecost, poured himself out abundantly upon the people of God. It is in this spiritual setting that we are experiencing a special day—first, with the meditation we have heard, and now, at the table of the Word and the Eucharist.

The Word of God in this celebration helps us to understand the mystery of the Church and, within it, of the Holy See, in the light of the two biblical images inspired by the Spirit in the Acts of the Apostles (1:12–14) and in the Gospel of John (19:25–34).

Let us begin with the fundamental account, which is the story of Jesus's death. John, the only one of the Twelve present at Calvary, saw and testified that beneath the cross stood Jesus's mother together with the other women (cf. Jn 19:25). And he heard with his own ears the last words of the Master, among which were these: "Woman, here is your son!," and then, turning to him, "Here is your mother!" (Jn 19:26, 27).

Mary's motherhood through the mystery of the Cross took an unimaginable leap: The mother of Jesus became the new Eve, the source of new and eternal life for every person who comes into the world, because her Son associated her with his redemptive death. The theme of fruitfulness is clearly present in this liturgy. The opening prayer immediately highlighted this by asking the Father that the Church, sustained by the love of Christ, "may be more fruitful day by day."*

The fruitfulness of the Church is the same fruitfulness as Mary's; it is realized in the lives of her mem-

---

* Roman Calendar, *Collect*, Memorial of the Blessed Virgin Mary as Mother of the Church on the Day After Pentecost.

bers to the extent that they relive, "in miniature," what the Mother lived, namely, they love according to the love of Jesus. All the fruitfulness of the Church and of the Holy See depends on the Cross of Christ. Otherwise, it is only appearance, if not worse. A great contemporary theologian wrote, "If the Church is the tree that grew from the tiny mustard seed of the cross, this tree is destined to produce mustard seeds in turn, and therefore fruits that repeat the shape of the cross, because it is precisely to the cross that they owe their existence."*

In the Collect, we also prayed that the Church may exult "in the holiness of her children." In fact, the fruitfulness of Mary and of the Church are inextricably linked to their holiness, which is their conformity to Christ. The Holy See is holy as the Church is holy, in her original core, in the very fabric of her being. The Apostolic See thus preserves the holiness of its roots while being preserved by them. But it is no less true that it also lives in the holiness of each of its members. Therefore, the best way to serve

---

* H. U. von Balthasar, *Cordula ovverosia il caso serio* (Brescia, 1969), 45–46.

the Holy See is to strive for holiness, each according to his or her particular state of life and the work entrusted to him or her.

For example, a priest who personally carries a heavy cross because of his ministry, yet every day goes to the office and tries to do his job to the best of his ability with love and faith, this priest participates in and contributes to the fruitfulness of the Church. Similarly, a father or mother of a family who lives in a difficult situation at home, with a child who is cause for concern or a sick parent, and continues his or her work with commitment, that man or woman is fruitful with the fruitfulness of Mary and of the Church.

Let us now turn to the second image, the one described by Saint Luke at the beginning of the Acts of the Apostles, which depicts the mother of Jesus together with the apostles and disciples in the Upper Room (1:12–14). It presents Mary's motherhood toward the nascent Church, an "archetypal" motherhood that remains relevant in every time and place. It is always and above all the fruit of the Paschal Mystery, of the gift of the Crucified and Risen Lord.

The Holy Spirit, who descends with power upon the first community, is the same Spirit that Jesus bestowed with his last breath (cf. Jn 19:30). This biblical image is inseparable from the first. The fruitfulness of the Church is always linked to the grace that flowed from the pierced heart of Jesus, together with blood and water, symbolizing the sacraments (cf. Jn 19:34).

In the Upper Room, thanks to the maternal mission she received at the foot of the cross, Mary is at the service of the nascent community: She is the living memory of Jesus, and as such, she is the center of attention that harmonizes differences and ensures the unity of the disciples' prayer.

In this text too, the apostles are listed by name, and as always, Peter is the first (cf. Acts 1:13). But he himself, in truth, is the first to be supported by Mary in his ministry. In the same way, Mother Church supports the ministry of Peter's successors with the Marian charism. The Holy See experiences in a very special way the coexistence of the two poles: the Marian and the Petrine. It is precisely the Marian pole, with its motherhood, gift of Christ and of the Spirit, that ensures the fruitfulness and holiness of the Petrine pole.

Dear friends, let us praise God for his Word, the lamp that guides our steps, even in our daily life at the service of the Holy See. Enlightened by his Word, let us renew our prayer: Grant, O Father, that your Church, sustained by the love of Christ, may be ever more fruitful in the Spirit, exult in the holiness of her children, and draw to her embrace all the whole human family.* Amen.

* Roman Calendar, *Collect*.

Be the Eyes of Peter

Address to Participants in the Jubilee and the Meeting of Pontifical Representatives

CLEMENTINE HALL

TUESDAY, JUNE 10, 2025

A special greeting to all of you, dear pontifical representatives. Before sharing the words I have prepared, I would just like to say to His Eminence and to all of you that what the Cardinal mentioned, I said not at the suggestion of anyone, but because I deeply believe it: Your role, your ministry, is irreplaceable. The Church would be unable to give many things if it were not for the sacrifice, the work, and everything that you do in order to enable such an important dimension of the great mission of the Church to proceed, and precisely in the case of which I spoke, namely the selection of candidates to the episcopate. Thank you from the heart for what you do! Now, please have a little patience.

After yesterday morning's celebration for the Jubilee of the Holy See, I am pleased to be able to stay briefly with you, the Pope's representatives to states and international organizations throughout the world.

First of all, thank you for coming, for undertaking a journey that for many of you was long. Thank you! You are already, as people, an image of the Catholic Church, since a diplomatic corps as universal as ours does not exist in any other country in the world. However, at the same time, I believe that one may equally say that no other country in the world has a diplomatic corps as united as you are—because your, our, communion is not merely functional, nor an idea; we are united in Christ and we are united in the Church. It is interesting to reflect on this fact: that the diplomacy of the Holy See constitutes in its very staff a model—certainly not perfect, but very meaningful—of the message it proposes: that of human fraternity and peace among all peoples.

Dear friends, I am taking my first steps in this ministry that the Lord has entrusted to me. And I also feel toward you what I confided some days ago, when speaking to the Secretariat of State: namely, my gratitude toward those who are helping me to carry out my service day by day. This gratitude is even greater when I think—and directly touch upon as I address various topics—that your work very often goes before me! Yes, and this applies in a particular way to you, because when a situation is presented to me that relates, for example, to the Church in a given country, I can rely on the documentation, reflections, and summaries prepared by you and your collaborators. The network of pontifical representations is always active and operative. This is for me a cause for great appreciation and gratitude. I say this thinking certainly of the dedication and organization, but, even more so, of the motivations that guide you, the pastoral style that should characterize you, the spirit of faith that inspires us. Thanks to these qualities, I too will be able to experience what Saint Paul VI wrote: that through his representatives, who reside in various nations, the Pope is able to participate in the very life of his sons and, almost by becoming part of it, becomes aware, in a surer and more rapid way, of their needs and at the same time their aspirations.*

---

* Cf. Paul VI, Apostolic Letter issued Motu Proprio *Sollicitudo Omnium Ecclesiarum*, Introduction, June 24, 1969.

And now I would like to share with you a biblical image that came to mind when thinking of your mission in relation to mine. At the beginning of the Acts of the Apostles (3:1–10), the story of the healing of the cripple describes the ministry of Peter well. We are at the dawn of Christian experience, and the first community, gathered around the apostles, knows it can count on a single reality: the Risen and Living Jesus. A crippled man sits begging at the door of the temple. It appears to be the image of a humanity that has lost hope and is resigned. Even today, the Church often encounters men and women who no longer have any joy, whom society has sidelined, or whom life has in a certain sense forced into begging for their existence. This page of Acts relates:

> Peter looked intently at him, as did John, and said "Look at us." He paid attention to them, expecting to receive something from them. Peter said, "I have neither silver nor gold, but what I do have I give you: in the name of Jesus Christ the Nazorean, [rise and] walk." Then Peter took him by the right hand and raised him up, and immediately his feet and ankles grew strong. He

> leaped up, stood, and walked around, and went into the temple with them, walking and jumping and praising God. (3:4–8)

The request Peter makes to this man—"Look at us"—makes us think. To look into one's eyes means to build a relationship. The ministry of Peter is to create relationships, bridges; and a representative of the Pope, first and foremost, serves this invitation to look into the eyes. Always be the eyes of Peter! Be men capable of building relationships where it is hardest to do. But in doing so, preserve the same humility and the same realism of Peter, who is well aware that he does not have the solution to everything: "I have neither silver nor gold," he says; but he knows he has what counts, namely Christ, the deepest meaning of every existence: "in the name of Jesus Christ the Nazorean, walk!"

To give Christ means to give love, to bear witness to the charity that is ready for everything. I am counting on you so that in the countries where you live, everyone may know that the Church is always ready for everything out of love, that she is always on the side of the last, the poor, and that she will always defend the sacrosanct right to believe in God, to believe that this life is not at the mercy of the powers of this world, but rather is traversed by a mysterious meaning. Only love is worthy of faith, in the face of the suffering of the innocent, the crucified of today, whom many of you know personally, as you serve peoples who are victims of war, violence, and injustice, or even of the false well-being that deludes and disappoints.

Dear brothers, may you always be consoled by the fact that your service is *sub umbra Petri* as you will find engraved on the ring that you will receive as a gift from me. Always feel you are bound to Peter, protected by Peter, sent by Peter. Only in obedience and in effective communion with the Pope may your ministry be effective for the edification of the Church, in communion with the local bishops.

Always have a blessing gaze, because the ministry of Peter is to bless, that is, always to know how to see the good, even that which is hidden, which is in the minority. Feel that you are missionaries, sent by the Pope to be tools of communion, unity, serving the dignity of the human person, promoting sincere and constructive relations everywhere with the authorities with whom you are required to cooperate. May your competence always be enlightened by the sound decision for holiness. The saints who were in the diplomatic service of the Holy See, such as Saint John XXIII and Saint Paul VI, provide an example to us.

Dear friends, your presence here today strengthens the awareness that the role of Peter is to confirm in faith. You are the first to need this confirmation in order to become its messengers, visible signs in every part of the world. May the Holy Door we all passed through together yesterday spur us to be courageous witnesses of Christ, who is always our hope. Thank you.

To Hope Is to Connect

Jubilee Audience

SAINT PETER'S BASILICA

SATURDAY, JUNE 14, 2025

I offer a warm greeting to all of you who are taking part in the Jubilee of Sport and in this international gathering on "The Momentum of Hope," sponsored by the Dicastery for Culture and Education. The time you spend together in these days will offer you a valuable opportunity to think about the relationship between athletic activity and the virtue of hope. When we think of it, sports are animated by hope, in the sense that they involve striving toward a goal, constantly trying to improve our performance, and learning to work with others as a team. At the same time, our deepest hopes challenge us to make the world of sports an arena where authentically human and Christian values can be exercised and communicated to others for the building of a better world. In the spirit of this Jubilee, then, I encourage you, and also the participants in the International Motorbike Rally, each in your own way, to be "missionaries of hope," working to bring about a culture of ever greater solidarity, acceptance, and fraternity. To all of you I cordially impart my blessing.

This morning we take up the series of catecheses on the Jubilee theme of hope begun by Pope Francis earlier this year. Like Jesus himself, God and man, the evangelical virtue of hope connects heaven and earth, our world and the kingdom of heaven. We see this reflected in the life of Saint Irenaeus of Lyon, a great bishop and theologian of the second century. Irenaeus was born in Asia Minor, nurtured in its apostolic traditions, and migrated to Europe as a missionary of the Gospel. His ministry was above all one of unity, grounded in the person of Jesus himself, true God and true man. By taking on our flesh, Jesus united us to one another, reconciling divisions and charging us to acknowledge him in all our brothers and sisters, especially the poor and those in need. Inspired by this teaching of Saint Irenaeus, may we work together for unity in our communities, opening doors and building bridges in place of walls. In this way, as pilgrims of hope, may we bear living witness to the Gospel message of unity, reconciliation, and peace in Christ.

Called to Be a Light of Hope

Video Message to the Young People of Chicago and the Whole World Gathered in Rate Field

SATURDAY, JUNE 14, 2025

It's a pleasure for me to greet all of you gathered together at White Sox Park on this great celebration as a community of faith in the Archdiocese of Chicago. A special greeting to Cardinal Cupich, to the auxiliary bishops, to all my friends who are gathered today on this, the feast of the Most Holy Trinity. And I begin with that because the Trinity is a model of God's love for us. God: Father, Son, and Spirit. Three persons in one God live united in the depth of love, in community, sharing that communion with all of us. So, as you gather today in this great celebration, I want to express both my gratitude to you and also an encouragement to continue to build up community, friendship, as brothers and sisters in your daily lives, in your families, in your parishes, in the archdiocese, and throughout our world.

I'd like to send a special word of greeting to all the young people—those of you gathered together today, and many of you who are perhaps watching this greeting through technological means, on the internet. As you grow up together, you may realize, especially having lived through the time of the pandemic, times of isolation, great difficulty, sometimes even difficulties in your families, or in our world today. Sometimes it may be that the context of your life has not given you the opportunity to live the faith, to live as participants in a faith community, and I'd like to take this opportunity to invite each one of you to look into your own hearts, to recognize that God is present and that, perhaps in many different ways, God is reaching out to you, calling you, inviting you to know his Son Jesus Christ, through the Scriptures, perhaps through a friend or a relative, a grandparent, who might be a person of faith. But to discover how important it is for each one of us to pay attention to the presence of God in our own hearts, to that longing for love in our lives, for searching, a true searching, for finding the ways that we may be able to do something with our own lives to serve others.

And in that service to others we may find that

coming together in friendship, building up community, we too can find true meaning in our lives. Moments of anxiety, of loneliness—so many people who suffer from different experiences of depression or sadness, they can discover that the love of God is truly healing, that it brings hope, and that actually, coming together as friends, as brothers and sisters, in community, in a parish, in an experience of living our faith together, we can find that the Lord's grace, that the love of God can truly heal us, can give us the strength that we need, can be the source of that hope that we all need in our lives. To share that message of hope with one another—in outreach, in service, in looking for ways to make our world a better place—gives true life to all of us and is a sign of hope for the whole world.

To, once again, the young people who are gathered here, I'd like to say that you are the promise of hope for so many of us. The world looks to you, as you look around yourselves, and says: We need you, we want you to come together to share with us in this common mission, as Church and in society, of announcing a message of true hope and of promoting peace, promoting harmony, among all peoples.

We have to look beyond our own—if you will—egotistical ways. We have to look for ways of coming together and promoting a message of hope. Saint Augustine says to us that if we want the world to be a better place, we have to begin with ourselves, we have to begin with our own lives, our own hearts.*

And so, in this sense, as you gather together as a faith community, as you celebrate in the Archdiocese of Chicago, as you offer your own experience of joy and of hope, you can find out, you can discover that you, too, are indeed beacons of hope. That light, that perhaps on the horizon is not very easy to see, and yet, as we grow in our unity, as we come together in communion, we can discover that that light will grow brighter and brighter. That light which is indeed our faith in Jesus Christ. And we can become that message of hope, to promote peace and unity throughout our world. We all live with many questions in our hearts. Saint Augustine speaks so often of our "restless" hearts and says, "Our hearts are restless until they rest in you, O God."† That restlessness is

* Cf. Saint Augustine of Hippo, *Sermons*, 311; and *Comment on St. John's Gospel, Homily*, 77.

† Saint Augustine of Hippo, *Confessions* I, 1,1.

not a bad thing, and we shouldn't look for ways to put out the fire, to eliminate or even numb ourselves to the tensions that we feel, the difficulties that we experience. We should rather get in touch with our own hearts and recognize that God can work in our lives, through our lives, and through us reach out to other people.

And so I'd like to conclude this brief message to all of you with an invitation to be, indeed, that light of hope. "Hope does not disappoint," Saint Paul tells us in his letter to the Romans (5:5). When I see each and every one of you, when I see how people gather together to celebrate their faith, I discover myself how much hope there is in the world. In this Jubilee Year of Hope, Christ, who is our hope, indeed calls all of us to come together, that we might be that true living example: the light of hope in the world today. So I would like to invite all of you to take a moment, to open up your own hearts to God, to God's love, to that peace which only the Lord can give us. To feel how deeply beautiful, how strong, how meaningful the love of God is in our lives. And to recognize that while we do nothing to earn God's love, God in his own generosity continues to pour out his love upon us. And as he gives us his love, he only asks us to be generous and to share what he has given us with others.

May you indeed be blessed as you gather together for this celebration. May the Lord's love and peace come upon each and every one of you, upon your families, and may God bless all of you, so that you might always be beacons of hope, a sign of hope and peace throughout our world. And may the blessing of Almighty God, the Father, the Son, and the Holy Spirit come upon you and remain with you always. Amen.

A Dance of Mutual Love

Homily for the Holy Mass in the Solemnity of the Holy Trinity, Jubilee of Sport

SAINT PETER'S BASILICA

SUNDAY, JUNE 15, 2025

In the first reading we heard these words:

Thus says the wisdom of God:The Lord possessed me, the beginning of his ways,
the forerunner of his prodigies of long ago;

. . . .

When the Lord established the heavens I was there
. . . then was I beside him as his craftsman,
and I was his delight day by day,
playing before him all the while,
playing on the surface of his earth;
and I found delight in the human race. (Prv 8:22, 27, 30–31)

For Saint Augustine, the Trinity and wisdom are intimately connected. Divine wisdom is revealed in the Most Holy Trinity, and wisdom always leads us to truth. While we are celebrating today the Solemnity of the Most Holy Trinity, we are also marking the Jubilee of Sport. This combination of Trinity and sport is somewhat unusual, yet the juxtaposition is not inappropriate. Every good and worthwhile human activity is in some way a reflection of God's infinite beauty, and sport is certainly one of these. For God is not immobile and closed in on himself, but is activity, communion, a dynamic relationship between the Father, the Son, and the Holy Spirit, which opens up to humanity and to the world. Theologians speak of *perichoresis*: The life of God is a kind of "dance"—a dance of mutual love.

This dynamism of God's inner life gives birth to life. We were created by a God who finds joy in giving existence to his creatures, who "delights" in our world, as we heard in the first reading (cf. Prv 8:30–31). Some fathers of the Church go so far as to speak of a *Deus ludens*, a God who "plays."* Sport can thus help us to encounter the Triune God, because it challenges us to relate to others and with others, not only outwardly but also, and above all, interi-

* Cf. Saint Salonius of Geneva, *In Parabolas Salomonis Expositio Mystica*; and Saint Gregory Nazianzen, *Carmina* I, 2, 589.

orly. Otherwise, sport becomes nothing more than an empty competition of inflated egos.

Here in Italy, spectators at sporting events often cheer athletes on by shouting out, "*Dai!*" (Come on!). The Italian word, however, means, literally, "Give!" This can give us cause to reflect. Sports are not only about physical achievements, however extraordinary, but also about giving of ourselves, putting ourselves "in play." It is about giving of ourselves for others—for our personal improvement, for our athletic supporters, for our loved ones, our coaches and colleagues, for the greater public, and even for our opponents. Being a "good sport" is more important than winning or not. Saint John Paul II—himself, as we know, a sportsman—put it this way: "Sport is joy of life, a game, a celebration. As such, it must be fostered . . . by recovering its sheer gratuity, its ability to forge bonds of friendship, to encourage dialogue and openness toward others . . . quite apart from the harsh laws of production and consumption and all other purely utilitarian and hedonistic approaches to life."*

---

* John Paul II, *Homily for the Jubilee of Sports*, April 12, 1984.

From this standpoint, let us reflect on three particular things that make sport, nowadays, a precious means for training in human and Christian virtues.

First, in a society marked by *solitude*, where radical individualism has shifted the emphasis from "us" to "me," resulting in a deficit of real concern for others, sport—especially team sports—teaches the value of cooperating, working together, and sharing. These, as we said, are at the very heart of God's own life (cf. Jn 16:14–15). Sport can thus become an important means of reconciliation and encounter: between peoples and within communities, schools, workplaces, and families.

Second, in an increasingly *digital society*, where technology brings distant people closer together, yet often creates distances between those who are physically close, sport proves a valuable and concrete means of bringing individuals together, providing a healthier sense of the body, of space, effort, and real time. It counters the temptation to escape into virtual worlds and it helps to preserve a healthy contact with nature and with real life, where genuine love is experienced (cf. 1 Jn 3:18).

Third, in our *competitive society*, where it seems that

only the strong and winners deserve to live, sport also teaches us how to lose. It forces us, in learning the art of losing, to confront one of the deepest truths of our human condition: our fragility, our limitations, and our imperfections. This is important, because it is through the experience of these limits that we open our hearts to hope. Athletes who never make mistakes, who never lose, do not exist. Champions are not perfectly functioning machines, but real men and women, who, when they fall, find the courage to get back on their feet. Saint John Paul II hit the mark when he said that Jesus is "the true athlete of God" because he defeated the world not by strength, but by the fidelity of love.*

It is no coincidence that sport has played a significant role in the lives of many saints in our day, both as a personal discipline and as a means of evangelization. We can think of Blessed Pier Giorgio Frassati, the patron saint of athletes, who will be canonized later this year on September 7. His straightforward and luminous life reminds us that, just as no one is

* John Paul II, *Homily at the Mass for the Jubilee of Sportsmen and Sportswomen*, October 29, 2000.

born a champion, no one is born a saint. It is daily training in love that brings us closer to final victory (cf. Rom 5:3–5) and enables us to contribute to the building of a new world. Saint Paul VI also observed this, twenty years after the end of the Second World War, when he reminded the members of a Catholic athletic association how much sports had helped to restore peace and hope in a society devastated by the consequences of war. He went on to say, "Your efforts are directed at the formation of a new society . . . , in the recognition that sport, by virtue of the sound educational values it promotes, can be a most useful means for the spiritual elevation of the human person, the primary and indispensable condition for an orderly, peaceful and constructive society."*

Dear athletes, the Church entrusts you with a beautiful mission: to reflect in all your activities the love of the Triune God, for your own good and for that of your brothers and sisters. Carry out this mission with enthusiasm: as athletes, as trainers, as associations and groups, and within your families. Pope

* Paul VI, *Address to the Members of the C.S.I.*, March 20, 1965.

Francis liked to point out that the Gospel presents the Virgin Mary as ever active, on the move, even "running" (cf. Lk 1:39), ever ready, as mothers are, to set out at a sign from God to help her children.* Let us ask her to accompany our effort and enthusiasm, and to guide it always toward the greatest victory of all: the prize of eternal life on that playing field where games will never end and our joy will be complete (cf. 1 Cor 9:24–25; 2 Tm 4:7–8).

* Cf. Francis, *Address to the Volunteers of World Youth Day*, August 6, 2023.

Share the Joy of the Universe

Address to the Participants of the Summer School of Astrophysics Promoted by the Vatican Observatory

CONSISTORY HALL

MONDAY, JUNE 16, 2025

I am pleased to have this opportunity to greet all of you, students and scholars from various parts of the world who are taking part in the Vatican Observatory Summer School. I offer you my prayerful good wishes that this experience of living and studying together will not only be academically and personally enriching, but also help you to develop friendships and forms of collaboration that can only contribute to the progress of science in the service of our one human family.

This year's summer school—I am told—is devoted to the theme "Exploring the Universe with the James Webb Space Telescope." Surely, this must be an exciting time to be an astronomer! Thanks to that truly remarkable instrument, for the first time we are able to peer deeply into the atmosphere of exoplanets where life may be developing and study the nebulae where planetary systems themselves are forming. With Webb, we can even trace the ancient light of distant galaxies, which speaks of the very beginning of our universe.

The authors of sacred Scripture, writing so many centuries ago, did not have the benefit of this privilege. Yet their poetic and religious imaginations pondered what the moment of creation must have been like, when "the stars shone in their watches and rejoiced; and their Creator called them and they said, 'Here we are!,' shining with gladness for him who made them" (Bar 3:34). In our own day, do not the James Webb images also fill us with wonder, and indeed a mysterious joy, as we contemplate their sublime beauty?

The space telescope science team has worked hard to make these images available to the general public, for which all of us can be grateful. In a special way, though, all of you who are taking part in the summer school have been given the knowledge and training that can enable you to use this amazing instrument in order to expand our knowledge of the cosmos of which we are a tiny but meaningful part.

Of course, none of you has come to this point all by yourself. Each of you is part of a much greater community. Think of all the people over the past thirty years who worked to build the space telescope and its instruments, and those who worked to develop the scientific ideas that it was designed to test. Along with the contribution of your fellow scientists, engineers, and mathematicians, it was also with the support of your families and so many of your friends that you have been able to appreciate and take part in this wonderful enterprise, which has enabled us to see the world around us in a new way.

Never forget, then, that what you are doing is meant to benefit all of us. Be generous in sharing what you learn and what you experience, as best you can and however you can. Do not hesitate to share the joy and the amazement born of your contemplation of the "seeds" that, in the words of Saint Augustine, God has sown in the harmony of the universe.* The more joy you share, the more joy you create, and in this way, through your pursuit of knowledge, each

* Cf. Saint Augustine of Hippo, *De Genesi Ad Litteram* V, 23, 44–45.

of you can contribute to building a more peaceful and just world.

With these thoughts, my friends, I renew my thanks for your visit and I assure you of my prayers for you, your families, and your work, and upon all of you, I willingly invoke God's blessings of wisdom and understanding, of joy and peace. God bless you!

The Compass of Natural Law

Address to Members of the International Inter-Parliamentary Union

HALL OF BENEDICTION

SATURDAY, JUNE 21, 2025

I am pleased that we can meet in the context of the Conference of the Inter-Parliamentary Union, during the present Jubilee of Governments. I offer a warm greeting to the members of the delegations coming from sixty-eight different countries, and, in a particular way, the presidents of the respective parliamentary institutions. Politics has rightly been defined as "the highest form of charity," quoting Pope Pius XI.* Indeed, if we consider the service that political life renders to society and to the common good, it can truly be seen as an act of Christian love, which is never simply a theory, but always a concrete sign and witness of

* Pius XI, *Address to the Italian Catholic University Federation*, December 18, 1927.

God's constant concern for the good of our human family.*

In this regard, I would like to share with you this morning three considerations that I deem important in the current cultural context.

The first concerns your responsibility to promote and protect, independent of any special interest, *the good of the community, the common good*, particularly by defending the vulnerable and the marginalized. This would mean, for example, working to overcome the unacceptable disproportion between the immense wealth concentrated in the hands of a few and the world's poor.† Those who live in extreme conditions cry out to make their voices heard, and often find no ears willing to hear their plea. This imbalance generates situations of persistent injustice, which readily lead to violence and, sooner or later, to the tragedy of war. Sound politics, on the other hand, by promoting the equitable distribution of resources, can offer an effective service to harmony and peace, both domestically and internationally.

---

* Cf. Francis, Encyclical Letter *Fratelli Tutti* on Fraternity and Social Friendship, October 3, 2020, 176–192.

† Cf. Leo XIII, Encyclical Letter *Rerum Novarum*, May 15, 1891, 1.

My second reflection has to do with *religious freedom and interreligious dialogue*. This area has taken on greater significance in the present time, and political life can achieve much by encouraging the conditions for there to be authentic religious freedom and that a respectful and constructive encounter between different religious communities may develop. Belief in God, with the positive values that derive from it, is an immense source of goodness and truth for the lives of individuals and communities. Saint Augustine spoke of the need to pass from *amor sui*—egotistic, myopic, and destructive self-love—to *amor Dei*—a free and generous love, grounded in God and leading to the gift of self. That passage, he taught, is essential for the building of the *civitas Dei*, a society whose fundamental law is charity.*

In order to have a shared point of reference in political activity, and not exclude a priori any consideration of the transcendent in decision-making processes, it would be helpful to seek an element that unites everyone. To this end, an essential reference point is the *natural law*, written not by human hands,

---

* Cf. Saint Augustine of Hippo, *De Civitate Dei*, XIV, 28.

but acknowledged as valid in all times and places, and finding its most plausible and convincing argument in nature itself. In the words of Cicero, already an authoritative exponent of this law in antiquity, I quote from *De Re Publica*:

> Natural law is right reason, in accordance with nature, universal, constant and eternal, which with its commands, invites us to do what is right and with its prohibitions deters us from evil. . . . No change may be made to this law, nor may any part of it be removed, nor can it be abolished altogether; neither by the Senate nor by the people, can we free ourselves from it, nor is it necessary to seek its commentator or interpreter. And there shall be no law in Rome, none in Athens, none now, none later; but one eternal and unchanging law shall govern all peoples at all times.*

Natural law, which is universally valid apart from and above other more debatable beliefs, constitutes

* Cicero, *De Re Publica*, III, 22.

the compass by which to take our bearings in legislating and acting, particularly on the delicate and pressing ethical issues that, today more than in the past, regard personal life and privacy. The *Universal Declaration of Human Rights*, approved and proclaimed by the United Nations on December 10, 1948, is now part of humanity's cultural heritage. That text, which is always relevant, can contribute greatly to placing the human person, in his or her inviolable integrity, at the foundation of the quest for truth, thus restoring dignity to those who do not feel respected in their inmost being and in the dictates of their conscience.

This brings us to a third consideration. The degree of civilization attained in our world and the goals you are charged to achieve are now facing a major challenge in the form of *artificial intelligence*. This is a development that will certainly be of great help to society, provided that its employment does not undermine the identity and dignity of the human person and his or her fundamental freedoms. In particular, it must not be forgotten that artificial intelligence functions as a tool for the good of human beings, not to diminish them, not to replace them.

What is emerging is in fact a significant challenge, one that calls for great attention and foresight in order to protect, also in the context of new scenarios, healthy, fair, and sound lifestyles, especially for the good of younger generations.

Our personal life has greater value than any algorithm, and social relationships require spaces for development that far transcend the limited patterns that any soulless machine can prepackage. Let us not forget that, while able to store millions of data points and answer many questions in a matter of seconds, artificial intelligence remains equipped with a "static memory" that is in no way comparable to that of human beings. Our memory, on the other hand, is creative, dynamic, generative, capable of uniting past, present, and future in a lively and fruitful search for meaning, with all the ethical and existential implications that this entails.*

Politics cannot ignore a challenge of this magnitude. On the contrary, it is called to respond to many citizens who rightly look with both confi-

---

* Cf. Francis, *Address to the G7 Session on Artificial Intelligence*, June 14, 2024.

dence and concern at the issues raised by this new digital culture.

During the Jubilee of the Year 2000, Saint John Paul II indicated Saint Thomas More as a witness for political leaders to revere and an intercessor under whose protection to place their work. Sir Thomas More was a man faithful to his civic responsibilities, a perfect servant of the state precisely because of his faith, which led him to view politics not as a profession but as a mission for the spread of truth and goodness. He "placed his public activity at the service of the person, especially the weak and poor; he handled social disputes with an exquisite sense of justice; he protected the family and defended it with strenuous commitment; and he promoted the integral education of youth."* The courage he showed by his readiness to sacrifice his life rather than betray the truth makes him, also for us today, a martyr for freedom and for the primacy of conscience. May his example be a source of inspiration and guidance for each of you!

---

* John Paul II, Apostolic Letter issued Motu Proprio *Proclaiming Saint Thomas More Patron of Statesmen and Politicians*, October 31, 2000, 4.

Sharing Bread to Multiply Hope

Solemnity of the Most Holy Body and Blood of Christ Holy Mass, Procession, and Eucharistic Blessing

SAINT JOHN LATERAN SQUARE

SUNDAY, JUNE 22, 2025

Dear brothers and sisters, it is wonderful to be in the presence of Jesus. The Gospel passage we just heard attests to this; it recounts how the crowds spent long hours listening to him speak about the Kingdom of God and seeing him heal the sick (cf. Lk 9:11). Jesus's compassion for the suffering shows us the loving closeness of God, who comes into our world to save us. Where God reigns, we are set free from all evil. Yet even for those who accept the Good News brought by Jesus, the hour of trial comes. In that deserted place, where the crowds were listening to the Master, evening fell and there was nothing to eat (cf. Lk 9:12). The hunger of the people and the setting of the sun speak to us of a limit that looms over the world and every creature: The day ends, as does the life of every human being.

At that hour of need and of gathering shadows, Jesus remains present in our midst.

Precisely when the day is ending and hunger sets in, as the apostles themselves ask him to dismiss the crowds, Christ surprises us with his mercy. He feels compassion for those who are hungry, and he invites his disciples to provide for them. Hunger is not foreign to the preaching of the Kingdom and the message of salvation. On the contrary, it speaks to us of our relationship with God. At the same time, five loaves and two fish seem completely inadequate to feed the people. The disciples' calculations, apparently so reasonable, reveal their lack of faith. For where the Lord is present, we find all that we need to give strength and meaning to our lives.

Jesus responds to the appeal of hunger with the sign of sharing: he *raises* his eyes, *recites* the blessing, *breaks* the bread, and *feeds* all present (cf. Lk 9:16). The Lord's actions are not some complicated magical rite; they simply show his gratitude to the Father, his filial prayer, and the fraternal communion sustained by the Holy Spirit. Jesus multiplies the loaves and the fish by sharing what is available. As a result, there is enough for everyone. In fact, more than enough.

After all had eaten their fill, twelve basketsful were gathered up (cf. Lk 9:17).

That is how Jesus satisfies the hunger of the crowd: He does what God does, and he teaches us to do the same. Today, in place of the crowds mentioned in the Gospel, entire peoples are suffering more as a result of the greed of others than from their own hunger. In stark contrast to the dire poverty of many, the amassing of wealth by a few is the sign of an arrogant indifference that produces pain and injustice. Rather than sharing, it squanders the fruits of the Earth and human labor. Especially in this Jubilee Year, the Lord's example is a yardstick that should guide our actions and our service: We are called to share our bread, to multiply hope, and to proclaim the coming of God's Kingdom.

In saving the crowds from hunger, Jesus proclaims that he will save everyone from death. That is the mystery of faith, which we celebrate in the sacrament of the Eucharist. For just as hunger is a sign of our radical needs in this life, so breaking bread is a sign of God's gift of salvation.

Dear friends, Christ is God's answer to our human hunger, because his Body is the bread of eternal life: Take this and eat of it, all of you! Jesus's invitation reflects our daily experience: In order to remain alive, we need to nourish ourselves with life, drawing it from plants and animals. Yet eating something dead reminds us that we, too, no matter how much we eat, will one day die. On the other hand, when we partake of Jesus, the living and true Bread, we live for him. By offering himself completely, the Crucified and Risen Lord delivers himself into our hands, and we realize that we were made to partake of God. Our hungry nature bears the mark of a need that is satisfied by the grace of the Eucharist. As Saint Augustine writes, Christ is truly "*panis qui reficit, et non deficit; panis qui sumi potest, consumi non potest*": He is bread that restores and does not run short; bread that can be eaten but not exhausted.* The Eucharist, in fact, is the true, real, and substantial presence of the Savior,† who transforms bread into himself in order to transform us into himself. Living and life-giving, the *Corpus Domini* makes us, the Church herself, the Body of the Lord.

For this reason, echoing the Apostle Paul (cf. 1

* Saint Augustine of Hippo, *Sermons*, 130, 2.
† Cf. *Catechism of the Catholic Church*, 1413.

Cor 10:17), the Second Vatican Council teaches that "in the sacrament of the Eucharistic bread, the unity of believers, who form one body in Christ, is both expressed and achieved. All are called to this union with Christ, who is the light of the world, from whom we come, through whom we live, and towards whom we direct our lives."* The procession that we are about to undertake is a sign of that journey. Together, as shepherds and flock, we will feed on the Blessed Sacrament, adore him, and carry him through the streets. In doing so, we will present him before the eyes, the consciences, and the hearts of the people—to the hearts of those who believe, so that they may believe more firmly; to the hearts of those who do not believe, so that they may reflect on the hunger present within them and the bread that alone can satisfy it. Strengthened by the food that God gives us, let us bring Jesus to the hearts of all, because Jesus involves everyone in his work of salvation by calling each of us to sit at his table. Blessed are those who are called, for they become witnesses of this love!

* Vatican II, Dogmatic Constitution on the Church *Lumen Gentium*, November 21, 1964, 3.

Loving with the Heart of Christ

Meditation on the Jubilee of Seminarians

SAINT PETER'S BASILICA, ALTAR OF CONFESSION

TUESDAY, JUNE 24, 2025

I am very pleased to meet you and to thank you all, seminarians and formators, for your warm presence. Thank you first of all for your joy and this enthusiasm of yours. Thank you, because with your energy you fan the flame of hope in the life of the Church! Today you are not only *pilgrims*, but also *witnesses of hope*: You bear witness to me and to everyone, because you have allowed yourselves to be involved in the fascinating adventure of the priestly vocation in a time that is not easy. You have accepted the calling to become meek and strong proclaimers of the Word that saves, serving an open Church and an outgoing missionary Church.

(And I will also say a word in Spanish: Thank you for courageously accepting the Lord's invitation to follow him, to be disciples, to enter the seminary. You need to be courageous, and do not be afraid!)

You are saying "yes" to Christ who calls to you, with humility and courage; and this "Here I am" that you say to him germinates within the life of the Church and lets itself be accompanied by the necessary path of discernment and formation. Jesus, as you know, calls you first and foremost to live an experience of friendship with him, and with companions on the journey (cf. Mk 3:13)—an experience destined to grow in a permanent way, even after ordination, and that affects all aspects of life. Indeed, there is no part of you that must be discarded, but everything must be taken on and transfigured according to the logic of the grain of wheat in the Gospel, in order for you to become happy people and priests, "bridges" and not obstacles to the encounter with Christ for all those who approach you. Yes, he must grow and we must shrink, so that we can be shepherds following his Heart.*

With regard to the Heart of Jesus Christ, how can

---

* Cf. John Paul II, Apostolic Exhortation *Pastores Dabo Vobis* on the Formation of Priests in the Circumstances of the Present Day, March 25, 1992, 43.

we fail to remember the encyclical *Dilexit Nos*, given to us by beloved Pope Francis?* Precisely in this time that you are living, namely, the time of formation and discernment, it is important to focus attention on the center, on the "motor" of your entire journey: the heart! The seminary, however it is conceived, should be a school of the affections. Today, in a special way, in a social and cultural context marked by conflict and narcissism, we need to learn how to love, and to do so like Jesus.†

Just as Christ loved with the heart of a man,‡ you are called to love with the Heart of Christ! *Amar con el corazón de Jesús.* But to learn this art, it is necessary to work on one's inner self, where God makes his voice heard, and from where the most profound decisions emerge; but which is also the place of tension and struggle (cf. Mk 7:14–23), to convert so that all our humanity has the scent of the Gospel. The first work therefore must be done on the inner life. Remember well Saint Augustine's invitation to return

* Cf. Francis, Encyclical Letter *Dilexit Nos* on the Human and Divine Love of the Heart of Jesus Christ, October 24, 2024.

† Cf. ibid., 17.

‡ Cf. Vatican II, Pastoral Constitution *Gaudium et Spes* on the Church in the Modern World, December 7, 1965, 22.

to the heart, because there we find the traces of God. To descend into the heart can frighten us at times, because inside it there are also wounds. Do not be afraid to take care of it, to let yourselves be helped, because it is precisely from those wounds that the capacity to be close to those who suffer will be born. Without the inner life, not even the spiritual life is possible, because God speaks to us right there, in the heart. God speaks to us in the heart, we must know how to listen to him. Part of this inner work is also learning how to recognize the movements of the heart: not only the rapid and immediate emotions that characterize the spirit of the young, but above all your sentiments, which will help you to discover the direction of your life. If you learn how to know your heart, you will become increasingly authentic and will not need to wear masks. And the privileged road that leads us to interiority is prayer: In an age in which we are hyperconnected, it becomes more and more difficult to have the experience of silence and solitude. Without the encounter with God, we are not even able to truly know ourselves.

I invite you to invoke the Holy Spirit frequently, so that he may form in you a docile heart, capable of perceiving God's presence, also by listening to the voices of nature and of art, poetry, literature, and music, as well as the humanities.* In the rigorous commitment of theological study, know also how to listen with an open mind and heart to the voices of culture, such as the recent challenges of artificial intelligence and those of social media.† Above all, as Jesus did, know how to listen to the often silent cry of the small, the poor and the oppressed, and of so many, especially the young, who seek meaning for their lives.

If you take care of your heart, with daily moments of silence, meditation, and prayer, you will be able to learn the art of discernment. This, too, is an important task: learning to discern. When we are young, we carry within us so many desires, so many dreams and ambitions. The heart is often crowded, and we can feel confused. Instead, following the example of the Virgin Mary, our inner life must become capable of safeguarding and meditating, capable of

* On literature, cf. Francis, *Letter on the Role of Literature in Formation,* July 17, 2024; on the humanities, cf. Vatican II, Pastoral Constitution *Gaudium et Spes*, 62.

† Cf. Congregation for the Clergy, *Ratio Fundamentalis Institutionis Sacerdotalis,* The Gift of the Priestly Vocation, December 8, 2016, 97.

symballein—as the evangelist Luke writes (Lk 2:19, 51)—of putting together the fragments.* Looking at yourselves from the surface, and composing the fragments of life in prayer and in meditation, asking yourselves: What does what I am experiencing teach me? What is it saying to my journey? Where is the Lord leading me?

Dear friends, have a meek and humble heart, like that of Jesus (cf. Mt 11:29). Following the example of the Apostle Paul (cf. Phil 2:5ff), you can take on the sentiments of Christ, in order to progress in human maturity, especially affective and relational maturity. It is important, indeed necessary, from the time of seminary, to focus much on human maturity, rejecting all masquerade and hypocrisy. Keeping our gaze on Jesus, we must learn to give name and voice even to sadness, fear, anguish, and indignation, bringing everything into our relationship with God. Crises, limitations, frailties are not to be hidden; they are indeed occasions for grace and paschal experience.

In a world where often there is ingratitude and thirst for power, where at times the logic of rejection

* Cf. Francis, Encyclical Letter *Dilexit Nos*, 19.

seems to prevail, you are called to bear witness to the gratitude and gratuitousness of Christ, the exultation and joy, the tenderness and mercy of his Heart. To practice the style of welcome and closeness, of generous and disinterested service, letting the Holy Spirit "anoint" your humanity even before ordination. The Heart of Christ is animated by an immense compassion: It is the good Samaritan of humanity, and it says to us, "Go and do likewise" (Lk 10:37). This compassion impels him to break for the crowds the bread of the Word and of sharing (cf. Mk 6:30–44), giving a glimpse of the gesture of the Upper Room and the Cross, when he would give himself to eat, and says to us, "Give them some food yourselves" (Mk 6:37), that is, make your life a gift of love.

Dear seminarians, the wisdom of the Mother Church, assisted by the Holy Spirit, over the course of time always seeks the most suitable methods for the formation of ordained ministers, according to the needs of different places. In this endeavor, what is your task? It is that of never compromising, never settling, never being just passive receivers, but of being passionate about priestly life, living the present, and looking to the future with a prophetic heart. I hope that this meeting of ours may help every one of you to deepen your personal dialogue with the Lord, in which you will ask him increasingly to assimilate the sentiments of Christ, the sentiments of his Heart. That Heart that beats with love for you and for all humanity. I wish you a good journey! I accompany you with my blessing.

Dear Seminarians, I am glad to be able to accompany you this morning, on the occasion of your Jubilee, together with the priests who accompany you on your formative journey. You come from various Churches in the world, and have very diverse experiences of life, but in the Lord we all form a single body. Indeed, there is just one hope to which you are called, that of your vocation (cf. Eph 4:4). Today, at the tomb of the Apostle Peter and together with me, his Successor, you solemnly renew the faith of your Baptism. May this Creed be the root from which will grow the "Here I am" that you will say with joy on the day of your priestly ordination. May God, who has begun his work in you, bring it to completion.

See the Invisible

Meditation on the Jubilee of Bishops

ALTAR OF THE CATHEDRA
IN SAINT PETER'S BASILICA

WEDNESDAY, JUNE 25, 2025

I deeply appreciate the effort all of you have made to come on pilgrimage to Rome, since I realize how pressing are the demands of your ministry. Yet each of you, like myself, before being a shepherd, is a sheep, a member of the Lord's flock. So we too, even before others, are asked to pass through the Holy Door, the symbol of Christ the Savior. If we are to lead the churches entrusted to our care, we must let ourselves be profoundly renewed by Jesus, the Good Shepherd, in order to conform ourselves fully to his heart and to the mystery of his love. "*Spes non confundit*," "Hope does not disappoint" (Rom 5:5). How often did we hear Pope Francis repeat those words of Saint Paul! They became one of his trademark phrases, so much so that he chose them to be the opening words of the Bull of Indiction of this Jubilee Year.

We, as bishops, are the primary heirs of that prophetic legacy, which we must preserve and transmit to the people of God by our words and the way we live our lives. At times, preaching the message that hope does not disappoint means swimming against the tide, even in certain painful situations that appear to be hopeless. Yet it is precisely at those times when it becomes all the more apparent that our faith and our hope do not come from ourselves, but from God. If we are truly close to those who suffer, the Holy Spirit can revive in their hearts even a flame that has all but died out.*

Dear friends, a bishop is a witness to hope by his example of a life firmly grounded in God and completely devoted to the service of the Church. This will be the case only insofar as he is conformed to Christ in his personal life and in his apostolic ministry. The Spirit of the Lord will then shape his way of thinking, his feelings, and his actions. Let us stop for a moment and together consider a few aspects of this witness.

---

* Cf. Francis, Bull of Indiction of the Ordinary Jubilee of the Year 2025, *Spes Non Confundit*, May 9, 2024, 3.

First, the bishop is the *visible principle of unity* in the particular church entrusted to him. It is his duty to build communion among its members and with the universal Church by fostering the variety of gifts and ministries given for its own growth and for the spread of the Gospel. In this service, as in his entire mission, the bishop can count on the special divine grace conferred on him at his episcopal ordination. This grace sustains him as a teacher of the faith, a minister of sanctification, and a spiritual leader; it strengthens his commitment to the Kingdom of God, to the eternal salvation of souls, and to the transformation of history by the power of the Gospel.

The second aspect I would like to consider, again in the light of Christ as the model of the bishop's life, could be put this way: The bishop is *a man who lives the theological life*. In a word, he is a person completely docile to the promptings of the Holy Spirit, who fills him with faith, hope, and charity and fans them into flame amid the various situations and challenges of daily life. The bishop, then, is a *man of faith*. Here I think of that marvelous passage in the Letter to the Hebrews (cf. Heb 11), where the author lists an entire genealogy of "witnesses" of faith, beginning with

Abel. I think specifically of Moses, who was called by God to lead the people to the promised land, and who, we are told, "remained steadfast, as if seeing him who is unseen" (Heb 11:27). Here we have a magnificent portrayal of a man of faith: He is one who, by the grace of God, sees ahead, glimpses the goal, and perseveres in times of trial. Think of all the times that Moses interceded for the people before God. So too, the bishop in his church acts as an intercessor, because the Spirit keeps the flame of faith alive in his heart.

Then too, the bishop is a *man of hope*, since "faith is the substance of things hoped for, the evidence of things not seen" (Heb 11:1). Especially at moments of difficulty in people's lives, the bishop, by this theological virtue, helps them not to despair: not simply by his words, but by his closeness. When families are greatly burdened and public institutions fail to provide adequate support; when young people are disillusioned and fed up with empty promises; when the elderly and those with grave disabilities feel abandoned, the bishop is close to them, not offering easy solutions, but rather the experience of communities that strive to live the Gospel in simplicity and solidarity.

Faith and hope then come together in him as a *man of pastoral charity*. The whole life of the bishop, his entire ministry, diverse and multifaceted as it is, finds its unity in what Saint Augustine calls the *amoris officium*. Here his theological life is expressed and shines forth in the highest degree. Whether preaching, visiting communities, listening to priests and deacons, or making administrative decisions, all that he does is inspired and motivated by the charity of Christ the Shepherd. With the help of God's grace, drawn daily from the celebration of the Eucharist and his prayer, the bishop gives an example of fraternal love to his coadjutor or auxiliary, to the bishop emeritus, and to the bishops of neighboring dioceses, to the priests, his closest collaborators, particularly those experiencing moments of difficulty or illness. His heart is open and welcoming, and so is his home.

Dear brothers, this is the theological core of the life of a bishop. Centered on these aspects, and always awakened by the same Spirit, a number of other essential virtues can be added: pastoral prudence, poverty, perfect continence in celibacy, and human virtues.

Pastoral prudence is the practical wisdom that guides the bishop in his decisions, in his governance, in his relations with the faithful and with their associations. A clear sign of prudence is his exercise of dialogue as a style and method, both in his relationships with others and in his presiding over participatory bodies: in other words, in his overseeing of synodality in his particular church. Pope Francis taught us much in this regard, insisting with pedagogical wisdom on synodality as a dimension of the life of the Church. Pastoral prudence also enables the bishop to guide the diocesan community by cherishing its traditions and by promoting new directions and initiatives.

To bear witness to the Lord Jesus, the bishop lives a life of evangelical *poverty*. His is a simple, sober, and generous lifestyle, dignified and at the same time suited to the conditions of the majority of his people. The poor must find in him a father and a brother, and never feel uncomfortable in meeting him or entering his home. In his personal life, he must be detached from the pursuit of wealth and from forms of favoritism based on money or power. The bishop must never forget that, like Jesus, he has been anointed with the Holy Spirit and sent to bring good news to the poor (cf. Lk 4:18).

Together with material poverty, the life of the bishop is also marked by that specific form of poverty that is *celibacy and virginity* for the sake of the Kingdom of Heaven (cf. Mt 19:12). Here, it is not just a question of living as a celibate, but of practicing chastity of heart and conduct, and in this way living a life of Christian discipleship and presenting to all the authentic image of the Church, holy and chaste in her members as in her Head. He must be firm and decisive in dealing with situations that can cause scandal and with every case of abuse, especially involving minors, and fully respect the legislation currently in force.

Finally, the bishop is called to cultivate those *human virtues* that the Council Fathers also chose to mention in the decree *Presbyterorum Ordinis*. These are of great help to him in his ministry and in his relationships with others. They include fairness, sincerity, magnanimity, openness of mind and heart, the ability to rejoice with those who rejoice and to suffer with those who suffer, as well as self-control, delicacy, patience, discretion, great openness to listening and engaging in dialogue, and willingness to serve. These virtues, which each of us possess to a greater or lesser extent by nature, can and must be cultivated in conformity to the Lord Jesus, with the grace of the Holy Spirit. Dear brothers, may the prayers of the Blessed Virgin Mary and Saints Peter and Paul obtain for you and your communities the graces that you most need. In particular, may they help you to be men of communion, always promoting unity in the diocesan presbyterate. May every priest, without exception, sense the fatherhood, brotherhood, and friendship of his bishop. That spirit of communion encourages priests in their pastoral outreach and makes the particular church grow in unity.

Beloved, Chosen, and Sent by the Lord

Homily for the Holy Mass and Priestly Ordinations, Jubilee of Priests

SAINT PETER'S BASILICA,
ALTAR OF THE CONFESSION

FRIDAY, JUNE 27, 2025

Today, the Solemnity of the Sacred Heart of Jesus, the Day of Prayer for the Sanctification of Priests, we celebrate this Eucharist with great joy as part of the Jubilee of Priests. Before all else, dear brother priests, I wish to say a word to you, who have passed through the Holy Door to pray at the tomb of the Apostle Peter and to immerse your baptismal and priestly garments once more in the Heart of the Savior. For some of you, this is happening on a unique day in your lives: the day of your ordination. To speak of the Heart of Christ in this context is to reflect on the entire mystery of the Lord's incarnation, death, and resurrection, which is entrusted in a special way to us, so that we can make it present in our world. In the light of the readings that we have just heard, let us reflect on how we can contribute to this work of salvation.

In the first reading, the prophet Ezekiel describes God as a shepherd who watches over his flock, counting his sheep one by one. He seeks out the lost, binds up the wounded, and strengthens the weak and sick (cf. Ez 34:11–16). He thus reminds us, in this age of vast and devastating conflicts, that the love of God has no limits. We are called to let ourselves be embraced and shaped by that love, and to realize that in God's eyes—and our own as well—there is no place for division and hatred of any kind.

In the second reading (cf. Rom 5:5–11), Saint Paul reminds us that God reconciled us to himself "while we were still weak" (v. 6) and "sinful" (v. 8) and exhorts us to entrust ourselves, along a daily path of conversion, to the transforming power of his Spirit who dwells in our hearts. Our hope is grounded in the knowledge that the Lord never abandons us: He is always at our side. At the same time, we are called to cooperate with him, above all by putting the Eucharist at the center of our lives, inasmuch as it is "the source and summit of the Christian life."* Then too, "through the fruitful reception of the sacraments, and especially by the frequent practice of sacramental penance," and finally through prayer, meditation on God's word, and the exercise of charity, conforming our hearts ever more closely to that of "the Father of mercies."†

This brings us to today's Gospel (Lk 15:3–7), which speaks of the joy of God—and of every shepherd who loves in the manner of his Heart—at the return of even one of his sheep to the fold. We are called to exercise pastoral charity with a generous love, like that of the Father, and to foster in our hearts the desire that no one be lost (cf. Jn 6:39) but that everyone, also through our ministry, may come to know Christ and have eternal life in him (cf. Jn 6:40). We are called to deepen our closeness to Jesus‡ and to be a source of harmony in the midst of our brother priests. We do so by bearing on our shoulders

* Vatican II, Dogmatic Constitution on the Church *Lumen Gentium*, November 21, 1964, 11.

† Paul VI, *Presbyterorum Ordinis*, 18.

‡ Cf. ibid., 14.

those who are lost, granting forgiveness to those who have erred, seeking out those who have gone astray or been left behind, and caring for those who suffer in body or spirit. And to do all this in a great exchange of love that, flowing from the pierced side of the crucified Lord, embraces all people and fills the entire world. For, in the words of Pope Francis, "the wounded side of Christ continues to pour forth that stream which is never exhausted, never passes away, but offers itself time and time again to all those who wish to love as he did. For his love alone can bring about a new humanity."[*]

The priestly ministry is one of sanctification and reconciliation for the building up of the Body of Christ in unity.[†] For this reason, the Second Vatican Council exhorted priests to make every effort to "lead all to the unity of charity," harmonizing differences so that "no one . . . may feel left out."[‡] It also encouraged priests to remain united with their bishop and within the presbyterate.[§] For the more

---

[*] Francis, Encyclical Letter *Dilexit Nos* on the Human and Divine Love of the Heart of Jesus Christ, October 24, 2024, 219.

[†] Cf. Vatican II, *Lumen Gentium*, 7.

[‡] Paul VI, *Presbyterorum Ordinis*, 9.

[§] Cf. ibid., 7–8.

we are united among ourselves, the more we will be able to lead others to the fold of the Good Shepherd, and to live as brothers and sisters in the one house of the Father.

Saint Augustine, in a homily delivered on the anniversary of his ordination, spoke of the joyful fruit of communion that unites the faithful, priests, and bishops, grounded in the recognition that all of us are redeemed and saved by the same gracious mercy of God. It was in that context that he spoke the celebrated words: "For you I am a bishop, with you I am a Christian."*

In the solemn Mass inaugurating my pontificate, I voiced before the people of God my great desire for "a united Church, a sign of unity and communion, which becomes a leaven for a reconciled world."† Today, I share this desire once more with all of you. Reconciled with one another, united and transformed by the love that flows abundantly from the Heart of Christ, let us walk together humbly and resolutely in his footsteps, firm in faith and open to

* Saint Augustine of Hippo, *Sermons*, 340, 1.
† Leo XIV, Holy Mass for the Beginning of the Pontificate, May 18, 2025.

all in charity. Let us bring the peace of the Risen Lord to our world, with the freedom born of the knowledge that we have been loved, chosen, and sent by the Father.

Now, before concluding, I would like to say a word to you, dear ordinands, who in a few moments, by the laying on of hands of the bishop and a renewed outpouring of the Holy Spirit, will become priests. What I have to say is simple, but I consider it important for your future and for the future of the souls entrusted to your care. Love God and your brothers and sisters, and give yourselves to them generously. Be fervent in your celebration of the sacraments, in prayer, especially in adoration before the Eucharist, and in your ministry. Keep close to your flock, give freely of your time and energy to everyone, without reserve and without partiality, as the pierced side of the crucified Jesus and the example of the saints teach us to do. Remember that the Church, in the two thousand years of her history, has had—and today continues to have—wonderful examples of priestly holiness. From the earliest communities on, the Church has raised up priests who have been martyrs, tireless apostles, missionaries, and champions of charity. Cherish this treasure: Learn their stories, study their lives and work, imitate their virtues, be inspired by their zeal, and invoke their intercession often and insistently! All too often, today's world offers models of success and prestige that are dubious and short-lived. Do not let yourselves be taken in by them! Look, rather, to the solid example and apostolic fruitfulness, frequently hidden and unassuming, of those who, with faith and dedication, have spent their lives in service of the Lord and their brothers and sisters. Keep their memory alive by your own example of fidelity.

Let us now entrust ourselves to the loving protection of the Blessed Virgin Mary, Mother of priests and Mother of hope. May she direct and sustain our steps, so that each day we may conform our hearts more closely to that of Christ, the supreme and eternal Shepherd.

Ecclesial Communion and the Vitality of Faith

Homily for the Holy Mass and Blessing of the Sacred Pallium for the New Metropolitan Archbishops on the Solemnity of Saints Peter and Paul

SAINT PETER'S BASILICA

SUNDAY, JUNE 29, 2025

Today we celebrate two brothers in faith, Peter and Paul, whom we honor as pillars of the Church and venerate as patrons of the diocese and city of Rome.

The story of these two apostles has much to say to us, the community of the Lord's disciples, as we make our pilgrim way in today's world. Upon reflection, I would like to emphasize two specific aspects of their faith: *ecclesial communion* and the *vitality of faith.*

First, *ecclesial communion.* Today's liturgy reminds us how Peter and Paul were called to share a single fate, that of martyrdom, which united them definitively to Christ. In the first reading, we see Peter in prison awaiting judgment (cf. Acts 12:1–11). In the second reading, the Apostle Paul, also in chains, tells us, in a kind of last will and testament, that his blood is about to be poured out and offered to God (cf. 2 Tm 4:6–8, 17–18). Peter and Paul were both ready to lay down their lives for the sake of the Gospel.

Yet this communion of the two apostles in the one confession of faith was the conclusion of a long journey on which each embraced the faith and lived out his apostolate in his own particular way. Their brotherhood in the Spirit did not erase their different backgrounds. Simon was a fisherman from Galilee, while Saul was highly educated and a member of the party of the Pharisees. Peter immediately left everything to follow the Lord, while Paul persecuted Christians before his life-changing encounter with the Risen Christ. Peter preached mainly to the Jews, whereas Paul was driven to bring the Good News to the gentiles.

As we know, the two were at odds over the proper way to deal with gentile converts, so much so that Paul tells us that "when Cephas came to Antioch, I opposed him to his face, because he stood self-condemned" (Gal 2:11). At the Council of Jerusalem, the two apostles would once more debate the issue.

Dear friends, the history of Peter and Paul shows us that the communion to which the Lord calls us is a unison of voices and personalities that does not eliminate anyone's freedom. Our patron saints followed different paths, had different ideas, and at times argued with one another with evangelical frankness. Yet this did not prevent them from living the *concordia apostolorum*, that is, a living communion in the Spirit, a fruitful harmony in diversity. As Saint Augustine remarks, "the feast of the two Apostles is celebrated on one day. They too were one. For although they were martyred on different days, they were one."*

All this invites us to reflect on the nature of ecclesial communion. Awakened by the inspiration of the Spirit, it unites differences and builds bridges of unity thanks to the rich variety of charisms, gifts, and ministries. It is important that we learn to experience communion in this way—as unity within diversity—so that the various gifts, united in the one confession of faith, may advance the preaching of the Gospel. We are called to persevere along this path, following the example of Peter and Paul, since all of us need that kind of fraternity. The whole Church needs fraternity, which must be present in all of our

---

* Saint Augustine of Hippo, *Sermons*, 295, 7.7.

relationships, whether between laypeople and priests, priests and bishops, bishops and the Pope. Fraternity is also needed in pastoral care, ecumenical dialogue, and the friendly relations that the Church desires to maintain with the world. Let us make an effort, then, to turn our differences into a workshop of unity and communion, of fraternity and reconciliation, so that everyone in the Church, each with his or her personal history, may learn to walk side by side.

Saints Peter and Paul also challenge us to think about the *vitality of our faith*. In our life as disciples, we can always risk falling into a rut, a routine, a tendency to follow the same old pastoral plans without experiencing interior renewal and a willingness to respond to new challenges. The two apostles, however, can inspire us by the example of their openness to change, to new events, encounters, and concrete situations in the life of their communities, and by their readiness to consider new approaches to evangelization in response to the problems and difficulties raised by our brothers and sisters in the faith.

At the heart of today's Gospel lies the question that Jesus asked his disciples. Today he asks us that same question, challenging us to examine whether our faith life retains its energy and vitality, and whether the flame of our relationship with the Lord still burns bright: "Who do you say that I am?" (Mt 16:15).

Every day, at every moment in history, we must always take this question to heart. If we want to keep our identity as Christians from being reduced to a relic of the past, as Pope Francis often reminded us, it is important to move beyond a tired and stagnant faith. We need to ask ourselves: Who is Jesus Christ for us today? What place does he occupy in our lives and in the life of the Church? How can we bear witness to this hope in our daily lives and proclaim it to those whom we meet?

Brothers and sisters, the exercise of a discernment born of these questions can enable our faith and the faith of the Church to be constantly renewed and to find new paths and new approaches to preaching the Gospel. This, together with communion, must be our greatest desire. Today I would like to speak to the Church in Rome in particular, because it, above all, is called to be a sign of unity and communion, a Church on fire with vibrant faith, a community of disciples who testify to the joy and consolation of the Gospel wherever people find themselves.

In the joy of the communion that the lives of Saints Peter and Paul invite us to cultivate, I greet my brother archbishops who today receive the pallium. Dear brothers, this sign of the pastoral responsibility entrusted to you also expresses your communion with the Bishop of Rome, so that in the unity of the Catholic faith, each of you may build up that communion in your local churches.

I would also like to greet the members of the Synod of the Ukrainian Greek Catholic Church. I thank you for your presence here and for your pastoral zeal. May the Lord grant peace to your people!

And with deep gratitude, I greet the delegation of the Ecumenical Patriarchate, sent here by my dear brother, His Holiness Bartholomew.

Dear brothers and sisters, strengthened by the witness of the holy Apostles Peter and Paul, let us walk together in faith and communion and invoke their intercession upon ourselves, the city of Rome, the Church, and the whole world.